Inclusion in Schools

Making a difference

Rosemary Sage

network
continuum

Acknowledgements

In writing about differences, I have to acknowledge the inspiration from my husband, Geoff, daughter, Helen, and son, Luke. They display the biggest differences in personality, interests and lifestyle among a group of three that you are ever likely to meet. Getting them to agree on a goal, and collaborate to achieve this, has been my greatest challenge! They are three wacky, lively and intelligent beings that often dislike compromise, co-operation and collaboration, but at least life is never dull!

Published by Network Continuum Education
The Tower Building
11 York Road
SE1 7NX

80 Maiden Lane, Suite 704
New York, NY 10038

www.continuumbooks.com

© Rosemary Sage 2007

First published 2004

British Library Catalogue in Publication Data
A catalogue record for this book is available from the British Library.

ISBN: 978 185539 360 8 (paperback)

Library of Congress Catalogue in Publication Data
To come

Project Editor: Gina Walker
Design and Layout: Neil Hawkins
Illustrations: Barking Dog Art, Annabel Spenceley

At the time of going to press all addresses and contact details are correct; however they may change at short notice, especially email and website addresses.

Contents

Introduction

In my first village school, the only things that mattered were whether we were girls or boys and whether we lived in private houses as opposed to those belonging to the council. Children who were slow at their work were accepted and given less to do than the rest. Certainly none of our families originated from outside of the UK and there were 28 little white faces in my first class. Times change and so do circumstances. Recently, I worked in a North London school with literally '57 varieties' of different ethnic groups to sort and service!

Gone, also, are the times when we might occasionally sit and dream at our desks. There is work to do and up to 125 public tests looming in the distance. No longer do afternoons exist for pond dipping and maypole dancing, which are *my* favourite memories of school! My first exam was the eleven-plus and passing it was a miracle because there was certainly no pressure to perform in our learning establishment. Life was for living, not working. Fun came before facts!

Today, education is a very sophisticated and stressful business both for students and staff. The child of a friend of mine, who is exceedingly bright, wet the bed for three months before her Key Stage 2 tests. She was terrified of not making her expected grade. According to the national children's mental health charity Young Minds, up to 40 per cent of young people in inner cities have emotional and behavioural problems. There is a price to pay for making children achieve.

Nevertheless, the world of today demands more knowledge and skills of its citizens than it probably did in the past. Jobs are more *people-* than *product-*centred, as technology has largely removed labour-intensive operations. We need high levels of inter- and intrapersonal skills to cope. The workplace suggests that these are being neglected in the present drive for children to learn facts and pass tests.

This book looks at the many issues facing educators with their classes full of children from diverse backgrounds, displaying different characteristics and having varying personal and academic needs. With a policy of inclusion, we are now discouraged from grouping children according to abilities, requiring fresh teaching and learning approaches to cope with fast and slow learners. Dip between the covers here to find handy information and top tips that I hope will make your life easier and your students' study less stressful. If the agony of learning is reduced and the pleasure of teaching increased by just one small fraction, we shall have made a start in climbing the ladder of success!

Whether you are a teacher, teaching assistant, school counsellor, social worker, therapist, psychologist or other educator, provided that you have an interest in making education work, this book is for you. I have enjoyed researching and writing it, so hopefully you will gain pleasure and benefit from reading and reflecting on the content.

Rosemary Sage

Chapter One

What is difference?

Overview

Although they may be required to follow an externally prescribed curriculum with a 'one size fits all' philosophy, schools now embrace greater differences among students and staff than ever before. In order to cope successfully with such diversity, we need more knowledge and understanding of educational and social processes to act as a platform on which to build a wider range of personal skills to support learning. This chapter reflects on issues of diversity and educational provision as a background for dealing with learning differences and difficulties.

◆ Introduction

When my son was six and his sister seven, I took them canoeing for the first time. Luke leaped into his boat and shot across the lake before Helen had steadied her craft and stepped gingerly inside. Neither child had been taught to canoe but what a difference there was in their performance! Children bring to learning such varying interests, aptitudes, personalities and backgrounds, even in the same family, that supporting their various needs remains the educator's greatest challenge.

This book unpacks the many issues, faced on a daily basis, by those involved in education. It does so with the aim of reflecting more carefully on the process so that we can provide worthwhile experiences for all our students. In the chapters that follow, we look at features such as personality, intelligence, styles of learning, teaching and communicating, social class, gender, race, learning difficulties, views and values. We do so within the context of a rapidly changing and diverse society with two particular dimensions that have implications for those working with youngsters.

- ◆ The first of these dimensions is **ethnic background**. Fifty years ago, the non-white population of Britain was probably less than 50,000 (Peach, 1982). Now, at least 11 per cent of children in our schools overall have an ethnic background other than British and approaching 8 per cent have English as their second language (DfEE/QCA, 1999).

◆ The second dimension is **family pattern**. Fewer people now spend their childhood with biological parents and siblings in a traditional nuclear family. Recently, the Office for National Statistics (2003) announced that nearly half the children in England and Wales are not being brought up in a traditional family. In 1997, 22 per cent of children were born into non-married cohabiting unions compared with 2 per cent in 1977. Nearly one in four children is brought up in a lone-parent family, a figure that has doubled since the 1980s. More than one in four children will see their parents divorced before they reach the age of 16. More than one in ten dependent children live in a step-family, a rise from the one in 14 stated by Haskey (1996). Predictions are that serial marriage will become the norm in Britain in the next decade and more families will go through separation and restructuring than will stay together. Gay and lesbian families present a challenging new format for society because they differ from the heterosexual tradition (O'Donnell, 1999). Schools are confused about acknowledging diverse family types. Section 28 of the Local Government Act (1988) stipulated that homosexuality, as a family relationship, should not be promoted whereas government guidance says that this should not prevent objective discussion of the topic.

In addition, it is common for both parents to be in paid employment (Ferri and Smith, 1996) but an increasing number of lone carers find it difficult to get and keep jobs. Parents with disabled children are particularly under pressure (Beresford, 1995).

TASK: Find out family patterns in your class and evaluate what this means for planning and organizing teaching.

EXAMPLE: Mark's Year 3 class included one child from a same-sex family, seven from lone-parent homes as well as nine from step-families, meaning that half the class were in non-standard living patterns. He ensured that resource materials presented varieties of family type, and made time to discuss differences and similarities in living, so children could learn to appreciate diversity.

It is against a background of constantly shifting circumstances that children are educated, so we need to define the terms that describe difference, such as gender, race, social class, culture, ethnicity, disability, special educational needs and special/additional needs. The list below includes comments about problems associated with using these terms, as they are often a focus for debate and dissension.

◆ **Gender** is the male or female classification according to the physical attributes of each. Male/female stereotypes often dictate how boys and girls are treated and are frustrating for many children.

◆ **Race** is a biological concept, classifying people by common origin and broadly similar physical features. It is a word that throws up typical stereotypes and false assumptions.

◆ **Social class** defines families on the basis of parent occupation according to the Registrar General's classification. There has been some blurring of the categories over recent decades with the general shift away from industrial work and towards service occupations, and with more school leavers now entering higher education.

◆ **Culture** encompasses the traditions and lifestyle shared by members of a society, including their ways of thinking, feeling and behaving. The term assumes an unjustified high level of homogeneity and cohesion among its members.

◆ **Ethnicity** reflects membership of a distinctive social group. Distinguishing features include physical appearance, language, religious beliefs and practices, national allegiance, family structure and occupation (Thomas, 1994). The term fixes on particular aspects of identity and ignores others that might be important. Children from mixed marriages and those living in countries where they are not native often have difficulties with identity.

◆ **Disability** describes an impairment that renders a person less able to perform 'normally'. The term assumes a person- rather than a situation-centred approach. For example, wheelchair users may be viewed as having mobility problems but equally could be seen as being hampered by inappropriate building design.

◆ **Special educational needs (SEN)** is a term signifying that a child has a learning difficulty calling for particular provision. Learning difficulties are those beyond the average for the child's age and may result from disabilities (Education Act, 1996, section 312). In practice, the term can be divisive, as such children become subject to the SEN Code of Practice arrangements that set them apart from their peers (DfES, 2001).

◆ **Special/additional needs** defines a child from a social group whose circumstances or background are different from most of the school population. Language, culture, overt racism and socio-economic disadvantage are identified as special/additional needs without any implication that individual students may have learning difficulties in the same sense as SEN (Robson, 1989). The term is frequently confused with SEN, resulting in low expectations of this group of students and confusion in planning support.

TASK: Take a child in your class and locate the number of diverse groups to which she or he belongs, using the categories above. Which ones produce difficulties for the child?

EXAMPLE: Mina was an Anglo-Indian twelve year old with speech problems due to partial hearing. Her English father had died and her grandparents cared for her while her mother worked to support Mina and her brother. There was considerable tension among the grandparents due to differences in cultural rearing patterns. Speech problems produced most difficulty for Mina, closely followed by emotional insecurity due to family tensions. Mina gained useful support at school from her learning mentor, with whom she had opportunities to discuss feelings and needs. She received weekly help from a teacher for the hearing impaired and made great progress as a result of belonging to a Communication Opportunity Group, which helped her develop thinking and interaction skills to make the most of her abilities.

In modern society, people have complex identities and multiple roles, so labels can be misleading. Discrimination against minority groups can often be detected in processes, attitudes and behaviour. For example, in 1972, West Indian children represented only 1 per cent of students in mainstream schools, but nearly 5 per cent of those in special schools for the educationally subnormal (Tomlinson, 1984). They continue to be over-represented in schools for students with emotional and behavioural difficulties (Inner London Education Authority, 1984) and those excluded from education (Bourne and co-workers, 1995).

Such findings reflect a diverse society, varying in uneven ways across a range of dimensions. For example, a random count of children on the special needs register at three Leicester schools finds a distribution of 17, 34 and 45 per cent. Boys far outnumber girls in schools for students with emotional and behavioural difficulties but by a smaller amount in special provision for hearing or learning problems (Riddell, 1996). Similarly, children from working-class backgrounds are over-represented in schools for moderate learning difficulties but not in those for severe problems. In highlighting these issues, the intention is to promote a more reflective and integrated approach to management, so enhancing learning for all students within a range of educational contexts. This is the aim and the challenge!

TASK: What are the percentages of different groups in your class? What particular group demands most attention and how would you plan for it?

> **EXAMPLE:** Sue had a Year 8 class of 35, with 18 English children, four Japanese, ten Indian and three from Somalia. The latter group had only recently arrived in England and, although the children were very bright, they had considerable language problems. Their needs were met in a twice-weekly Communication Opportunity Group led by a teaching assistant where they joined nine other students. This gave them opportunities to learn to think and express themselves in a format where they were coached in appropriate interactive behaviour.

In meeting such aims and challenges, we have to examine our present educational system and the range of people who support it. Three philosophies have influenced teaching arrangements.

◆ **Segregation**: an approach based on the belief that students are best educated with others of similar ability. We witness this in the grammar school tradition and ability groupings in classes. Main tenets are *subject teaching, selection* and *standards of attainment.*

◆ **Integration**: an approach whereby children have a right to be educated alongside their peers, implemented when children in special provision were shifted into mixed ability, mainstream settings after the 1981 Education Act. Principles are *individualized learning* and *identification of special needs.*

◆ **Inclusion**: an approach going beyond the idea that all children should be educated in the same place, stressing equity and including everyone, if possible, in the curriculum. Major ideas are *participation, development of full potential* and *involvement of the wider community.*

Our present drive towards the process of inclusion is based on human equality and standard attainments. Tensions exist, however, because of personal variations in interests and abilities, and we must take these into account. Herrnstein (1973) encapsulates this clearly:

Belief in human equality leads to rigid, inflexible expectations, often doomed to frustration, thence to anger. Ever more shrilly, we call on educational and social institutions to make everyone the same, when we should be trying to mould them around the inescapable limitations and variations of human ability.

◆ Analysing your own school context

We have to acknowledge dilemmas when developing effective learning for our students. In attempting this, it is useful to begin with a Strengths, Weaknesses, Opportunities and Threats (SWOT) analysis to consider the issues that face us in our particular workplace. Jot these down in a grid arrangement, as shown below.

Strengths:	Weaknesses:
Opportunities:	Threats:

What did you come up with? Did your school's strengths include a strong leadership? Perhaps your weaknesses included a solid view *against* inclusion? Were there chances for training and reflection noted in your 'opportunities' box? Did you include among your 'threats' a massive workload with no space to review and revise? Everyone attempting this analysis will have different issues to face and fight in providing a stable learning base.

◆ Professionals involved in education

Next, we consider the wide range of people involved in providing educational support. In implementing inclusive policies, a variety of skills are needed. In school, not only do we need teachers with expertise in the curriculum, but also teaching assistants trained to help students access what is on offer. Learning mentors and counsellors assist students to come to terms with complex problems in their lives, which often interfere with the learning process. Curriculum managers are required to co-ordinate the assessment and review process and liaise with experts from the community. Outside professionals such as doctors, psychologists, therapists, specialist teachers and social workers may be involved in assessment and intervention of students with special needs. Finally, administrators are needed to create systems that cater for the delivery of complex procedures in schools.

Education is now a very sophisticated business with children, families, schools and the community as key stakeholders. An integrated approach to learning support takes account of the individual perspectives of each group. Social changes and legal reforms have affected their position in relation to one another; these aspects are reviewed here because of their implications for practice.

◆ Perspectives on education

Child perspectives

Although it seems evident that children's views should be taken into account over decisions made for them, this principle was not enshrined in English law until the 1989 Children Act. In 1991, the UK agreed to be bound by the United Nations Convention on the Rights of the Child, in which Article 12 states that a child who is capable of forming and expressing her views is given the opportunity to do so in matters affecting her. The SEN Code of Practice (revised 2001) has this as a fundamental principle (DfES, 2001, paragraphs 1.5 and 3.1). Schools have introduced arrangements for consulting and involving students. Rudduck and Flutter (2000) note that children can contribute greatly to thinking on how the curriculum is presented and how learning can be made more effective. Student views are commonly collected in a questionnaire such as the one on page 13.

TASK: Try this questionnaire with students at the end of each term. Pair up a reader with a non-reader, if necessary, so that all can participate and exchange views. Encourage the class to bring together some of the information so they are made aware of each other's learning experiences. Read Jelly and co-workers (2000) for more discussion on assessing student views.

Questions to record your views about school

Name: _____ Date: _____

Think about what you have done in school this term. Answer these questions.

1   What did you like doing most?

_____

2   What did you not like doing?

_____

3   What did you do best?

_____

4   What things were difficult for you?

_____

5   What things did you improve?

_____

6   What helped you to learn better?

_____

Now think about next term. Answer these questions.

1   What would you like to do better?

_____

2   What do you need help with?

_____

3   What worries you about school?

_____

4   Who would you like to talk to about your worries?

_____

Parent perspectives

The Organization for Economic Co-operation and Development (OECD) survey showed benefits of parent involvement in education across nine countries, including Britain, citing these reasons (Kelley-Laine, 1998):

- **Democracy**: the right of parents to be involved in education

- **Accountability**: participating parents ensure accountability

- **Choice**: parental choice of education meets needs more successfully

- **Standard**: improved home–school relations raise standards, confirmed by research

- **Disadvantage**: parent support helps to provide opportunities even for those from the most disadvantaged backgrounds

- **Social problems**: school–family programmes (drug/alcohol abuse; teenage pregnancy; crime) have positive effects

- **Resources**: parents provide unpaid staffing and funds for schools.

With regard to parent and professional involvement with SEN children, Cunningham and Davis (1985) describe three models of practice to examine relationships.

1. **Expert**: parents are passive recipients of expert knowledge and advice.

2. **Transplant**: some expertise can be transplanted to parents for carrying out activities with a child.

3. **Consumer**: parents are key decision makers, selecting information and services according to need.

TASK: What activities is it reasonable to expect parents to carry out in line with the 'transplant' model, above? What support do you need to give parents to carry these out successfully?

EXAMPLE: Andrew found it difficult to understand what he read. His teacher showed his mother how to approach the problem. A summary of the story was to be given to Andrew first, for him to tell back. The mother was primed to ask questions to help Andrew think beyond the facts presented. For example, in the story of 'The Three Little Pigs', she might ask 'What other ways could the pigs have got rid of the wolf?' Finally, the story was read and pictures made to pinpoint the main events and fix the place, people and happenings firmly in his mind.

The models are idealistic, as not all parents cope easily with 'transplant' and 'consumer' requirements. It is likely that all three apply at some time during parent–professional involvement. They are useful, however, in examining power relationships and contrast with a 'partnership' model in which teachers are viewed as being experts on education and parents as being experts on their children (Hornby, 1995). Even though parents are seen as partners, some relate to professionals more successfully than others. Rehal (1989) showed that some parents from ethnic minority communities had poor levels of communication and involvement with schools because different cultural backgrounds bring about misunderstandings. The public perceives that professionals and LEAs have been slow to embrace partnership ideas, and legislation has attempted to redress the power imbalance. The establishment of the SEN Tribunal was a major step in this direction (Education Act, 1993).

School perspectives

Up until 1989, the dominant voices in educational policy and practice in UK schools were teachers. This led to inconsistent educational standards across the land and was the impetus for the development of the national curriculum and Key Stage Assessments (DES, 1989), which removed the control educators had over what and how information was taught. The new ethos is more prescriptive and makes demands on teachers to push students to achieve requisite levels of attainment. Schools are thus accountable for the delivery of the curriculum in a very different way than before. The national curriculum aims to:

◆ give incentive for weak schools to catch up with achieving ones, while the latter are challenged to do even better

◆ provide teachers with precise objectives

◆ provide parents with clear, accurate information

◆ ensure continuity and progression

◆ focus schools on getting the best possible results from children.

Most teachers see sense in the new arrangements but feel the system is too rigid. Children's brains mature at different rates so that fixed expectations regarding performance hinder rather than help learning (Sage, 2000b). In Northern Ireland, and recently Wales, early Key Stage Assessments have been abandoned for this reason. An approach whereby children take the tests when ready for them is preferred. Nevertheless, national curriculum guidelines have raised educational expectations in the UK and given teachers a useful framework in which to plan their lessons.

Community perspectives

The school governing body includes representatives from the local community, and now has a firmer grip over school arrangements than ever before. There were concerns that a rigid curriculum with a 'one size fits all' policy could not fulfil the requirements of all students, particularly those with special needs (Upton, 1990). Tomlinson (2000) argued that the new emphasis on market forces and consumer choice would create disadvantages for 'undesirable customers', such as those with SEN, social class, race and ethnicity issues, who might prevent schools from reaching required levels on national league tables of performance. School improvement and effectiveness research, however, has found that schools showing gains also have a strong record of inclusion (Ainscow, 1995). Such schools support their staff in developing a wide range of responses to all students, and encourage the local community to help by becoming involved in pupil learning.

TASK: Use the Index for Inclusion (Booth and co-workers, 2000) to assess how your school is coping with issues of inclusion. All schools have been issued with the original version of the Index, which provides a checklist to evaluate the strengths and weaknesses of policies and practices.

◆ An integrated approach to learning

Providing successful student support, therefore, depends on developing an integrated approach that brings together children, parents, schools and communities in:

- ◆ providing education
- ◆ selecting relevant approaches
- ◆ employing research to assist development.

TASK: Consider these three dimensions of an integrated approach, and reflect on your own knowledge in these areas. Which aspect needs most attention from you? Locate the sections of this text that will help to inform you.

Educational provision

Successful performance is an outcome of the interaction between the individual characteristics of learners and the contexts in which they learn. To understand diversity, we have to consider the curriculum *and* learning context. An analysis of learning difficulties in English, for example, should incorporate curriculum demands and methods of teaching employed. The importance of this approach is widely recognized (SEN Code of Practice, DfES, 2001, paragraph 5.6) but not widely practised.

TASK: Consider a student with English as a second language and list difficulties, curriculum demands and teaching methods in English (or another relevant subject). Use a table with column headings as shown.

Learning difficulties	Curriculum demands	Teaching methods

For example, you might note in the difficulties column that the student has a limited vocabulary, whereas the curriculum demands suggest there are technical words to be learned in connection with English grammar (noun, adjective, verb, adverb, conjunction and so on) but the teaching method does not give much emphasis to this.

Goacher and co-workers (1988) stated that professional reports focus largely on deficits in the child with little attention given to the learning context. Recent work by Frederickson and Cline (1995) and Avramadis and Bayliss (1998) state that teachers focus solely on 'within-the-child' factors when seeking to explain learning problems. McKee and Witt (1990) suggested the reason is that professionals lack the knowledge and expertise required to identify other issues. This book aims to fill the gap by providing the knowledge that educators need to develop inclusion policies and practice.

Relevant approaches

Many approaches focus on certain aspects of learning difficulty and reduce these in artificial ways. Take a child who behaves badly. What is required for that child to behave better? Here are some ideas. The child must be able to:

◆ understand the norms for informal and formal social exchanges

◆ understand how rules for behaviour change across contexts

◆ know the behaviour expectations of any specific situation

◆ judge accurately the behaviour of others

◆ understand feedback and the way others perceive him

◆ control impulses and think out ways to respond well to others

◆ think out the consequences of different ways of behaving

◆ decide what is appropriate to say or do

◆ communicate feelings and views clearly and considerately

◆ cope with people she dislikes as well as those she likes.

What do you observe about this list? More is required than just knowing the social rules of behaviour and conforming to these. Thinking and communication are evident in perception, processing, problem solving, and expressive activities that underpin appropriate behaviour. An approach to controlling behaviour that combines behavioural, cognitive and communicative competences is suggested in order to tap into all the abilities needed. The Communication Opportunity Group Scheme (COGS) is an example of a holistic approach that encourages thinking and its expression, for personal and academic success, and takes account of the social context in which children and adults are interacting (Sage, 2000a and 2000b). It is important to foster relationship processes as Masters and Furman (1981) found that children were more skilful at interacting with those they liked than with those they disliked, which has obvious implications for classroom co-operation. Cooper (2001) reviews COGS in approaches that work with children experiencing social and emotional difficulties and commends its evidence base.

Research and practice

There has been extensive debate about the quality of educational research and its relevance to policy and practice. On the one hand, Hillage and co-workers (1998) suggest that we use more evidence-based decision making, whereas Hammersley (1997) concludes that:

> There is much wrong with the quality of teaching in schools but it seems that educational research can only play a fairly limited role in resolving problems.

Research analyses, highlights and provides understanding but remedying situations is a practical business that demands professional expertise. There are, however, parallels between the process of research providing evidence and the approach to assessment of difficulties described in the revised Code of Practice (DfES, 2001). This advocates:

◆ generating hypotheses about difficulties within and without the child (for example, student does not understand lessons – could be due to deafness, comprehension disorder, limited background knowledge, low intelligence, teacher communication style, and so on)

◆ collecting a range of data from different sources to test hypotheses (for example, hearing test, language and IQ assessment, observations, interviews and so on)

◆ reflecting on the validity and reliability of the collected information (for example, compare data sources over time and context)

◆ monitoring changes in student progress in response to action taken (for example, decide criteria to measure from base-line performance, record information at time intervals)

◆ evaluating the effectiveness of approaches (for example, locate improvements – where, when, how and so on).

TASK: Is there a child with special needs or special educational needs in your class? Use the approach described opposite to assess their difficulties and plan action.

Professionals who conduct this cycle of activities in relation to students find that it gives a research basis which involves participants and provides potential for illuminating outcomes. It would appear, therefore, that research does and should make a contribution to practice. Selection of appropriate strategies for helping students may be informed by evidence such as that cited by Paul Cooper (2001) on what works in specific kinds of situation. An application such as COGS (Sage, 2000a), to meet a particular need, has a theory of narrative thinking development for successful long-term improvement. There must also be systematic data collection to provide evaluation of a particular strategy in relation to objectives identified for students.

This is important because there have been many expensive schemes used with students that have not been based on sound knowledge of learning. These have petered out because they lacked evidence of effectiveness, which research provides. An example of this was a reading scheme, popular in the 1970s, based on a phonetic alphabet. This eliminated the problems of sound–letter inconsistencies that hinder some students' reading development. Although it made reading less of a problem initially, there were huge difficulties in making the transfer to conventional spellings at later stages. The scheme also ignored the fact that children acquire reading in normal situations such as poring over cereal packets and scrutinizing advertisements. Confusion between school and real-world demands resulted. Although many local education authorities made a big financial investment in the reading scheme and saw this as an answer to school failures, ten years later the whole strategy was dropped like a ton of bricks. It made reading more rather than less hazardous, as students had to learn one graphic system, then unlearn it to cope with orthodox written materials. Many made vociferous arguments against the method but were ignored.

◆ Review

This chapter has set the scene for considering differences that children bring to learning and the support that will be effective for their personal and academic success. Our society has a rich ethnic mix and a variety of interests and aptitudes among its members, which is both positive and problematic. In order to cope with such diversity we need to work towards an integrated approach to education that takes into account the perspectives of all stakeholders and aspects of the educational process. In the following chapters, we consider these dimensions in greater detail, starting in Chapter Two with aspects of personality and intelligence. So, let us get into the business of dissecting who and what we are as the basis for taking on a world of difference!

Main Points

- ◆ Children enter school with complex identities and multiple roles, which impact on learning.

- ◆ There is a tendency in some contexts for family and social patterns to be less stable than in the past, which has consequences for children's emotional, social and academic development.

- ◆ The drive towards inclusion creates opportunities but also threats because of its demands on schools.

- ◆ The perspectives of children, parents, schools and community need to be considered in making educational decisions.

- ◆ An emphasis on 'within-' rather than 'without-the-child' factors has mitigated against successful support for learning.

- ◆ An integrated teaching approach accounts for stakeholders' perspectives in educational provision, using theory and research to inform and deal with student differences more judiciously.

Chapter Two

What are personality and intelligence differences?

Overview

Personal characteristics and problem-solving skills are the survival kits that enable us to cope with both life and learning. Unpacking these human attributes gives us further insight into learning and teaching processes, and provides ideas to improve our management of individuals and groups.

Introduction

Let me introduce you to three 12 year olds in their first year in senior school. Yung Chan, is bright and bubbly with a keen interest in her work. Mark is tall, sporty and a born leader, who finds lessons a bit of a drag and is slow to meet his targets. Baljit is shy, keen to learn English and succeed in school, but finding it difficult to settle to work, being easily distracted by friends.

Here we have three delightful students with very different personalities, aptitudes and backgrounds. You can't see them, so you will not have noticed that Yung Chan wears hearing aids and Baljit is a right hemiplegic (paralysis of the right side of his body), resulting from birth injury.

These children slot into many different categories. Yung Chan is Chinese, highly gifted and has a severe hearing loss. Mark is English, a physically talented leader and emotionally stressed because his single mum has terminal cancer. Baljit is Indian and speaks Gujerati at home but struggles to learn English, as communication is not easy for him.

All students have differences separating them from their peers, and difficulties with which they have to grapple. Underlying their diverse circumstances are individual personalities and intelligences. What characteristics and aptitudes are revealed to others will depend entirely on the attitudes, values and support of their contexts. For example, if the environment is hostile, a child will withdraw or become aggressive and respond reluctantly. If the reverse is the case, and there is a pleasant atmosphere in place, the child is more likely to be content and co-operative. Children, however, bring social and emotional baggage from home into school, which complicates issues and may result in variable behaviour and performance.

◆ Personality

Personality refers to the many attributes that characterize us, such as shyness, patience, friendliness, aggression, impetuosity or persistence. When first starting teaching, I imagined that I would think of students in terms of their ability. I was soon put right – because it was the different dispositions of the members of my groups that made the overwhelming impact on me. I placed them into three categories:

- ◆ 'snaps'
- ◆ 'crackles'
- ◆ 'pops'.

The **snaps** are children who snap straight into action. They are keen to work and eager to please, needing little encouragement to send them racing. They represent only about 10 per cent of the class. They prefer to work alone because they can achieve more quickly. What are their characteristics? They are interested, attentive, persistent, determined, dedicated, independent, assertive, single-minded, to name but a few of their attributes! Indeed, they are the teacher's pets!

The **crackles** are the chatterers and listeners, always talking or attending to friends and finding it difficult to settle to work. There is generally something more interesting to consider, such as the latest shade of nail polish, last night's football scores or what is on at the multiplex. This group is the largest, with around 80 per cent of the class fitting this description! They prefer to work in groups, especially when they can negotiate the tasks. What are their characteristics? They are friendly, gregarious, popular, talkative, attentive listeners, easily distracted – in fact, out and out groupies!

The **pops** are students who pop up as leaders not only of sports teams but also of wild gangs! They have persuasive powers and patter, winning over their peers easily. They represent about 10 per cent of the class and may be on your side but also turn up as class rebels. Pops make good group leaders and like the chance to shine. What are their characteristics? They are visionary, organizing, communicative, competitive, empathetic, energizing, facilitating, charismatic – and watch out, because they can be bossy and demanding!

How do our 12 year olds match up to this framework? Well, Yung Chan is a 'snap', while Baljit is a 'crackle' and Mark is definitely a 'pop'! It may be naïve to regard them so, as circumstances change how we act, but categorization has a strong place in trait theory (the idea that we are born with certain dispositions to behave). Trait terms such as introversion (shyness) and extroversion ('outgoing-ness') are now in our everyday vocabulary (Eysenck and Eysenck, 1975).

Groups

The issue about personality is whether yours complements or clashes with classmates or colleagues. With maturity comes the more gracious acceptance of others and the desire to spend time with people who please rather than irritate. Nevertheless, we have to get on with quiet, shy, calm, noisy, boisterous or volatile people around us. The crucial thing is whether we can blend our personality into the group to which we belong.

The ways in which people interact in groups are called dynamics and by learning about these we can enhance our function. An inclusive school philosophy is dependent on our skills for working together in groups, but what are the benefits and the risks?

Benefits of groups	Risks of groups
Better results	Danger of someone being made a scapegoat if things go wrong
Efficient use of resources	Groups encourage unnecessary conformist behaviour
Individual responsibility for outcomes is minimized	Groups may induce apathy, boredom and withdrawal from participation
Groups encourage commitment	Personality clashes, conflict or competitive behaviour may be destructive
More risk-taking	Groups tend to function at the level of the lowest common denominator
Combined judgement helps to eliminate errors	Inappropriate dominance by some members
More creative solutions	Exclusion of those without the skills to discuss and negotiate successfully
Groups ease any sense of isolation and meet needs for belonging	If there is personality imbalance it is difficult for a group to function

Children and adults need to be aware of their own personalities and how they impact on others. A useful exercise is to ask people to match up everyone in their group with an animal and justify their choice. Below, and on the following pages, is the response of a student I know.

The lion is a leader.

The hedgehog is a stickler for the rules, and a bit prickly and awkward.

The deer is shy and retiring and not very confident about trying new things.

The sheep follows the crowd, unquestioning.

The horse is willing, amenable and dependable.

The pig is a stick-in-the-mud, dislikes change and often argues or grunts away.

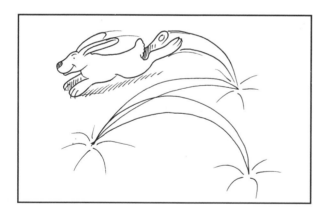

The giraffe views things in ways that others cannot, but is not assertive and is often ignored.

The rabbit jumps around and never settles on a decision.

The kitten is soft, sympathetic and comforting, and is good at helping others settle arguments.

These are interesting ideas that are well worth exploring with children, and help them to consider how to work effectively with others.

TASK: Jot down reasons why a group works well, from your experience. Compare it with the list below. What are the similarities and differences?

To function well, a group needs:

- ◆ a common purpose that is clearly understood by everyone
- ◆ organization that enables the purpose to be achieved
- ◆ clear roles for participants that are acceptable to them
- ◆ clear boundaries that set behaviour required to fulfil the purpose
- ◆ capacity to absorb and lose members without losing identity
- ◆ capacity to adapt, build and grow without losing direction
- ◆ freedom from cliques that might subvert the purpose
- ◆ value for each individual's contribution to help acceptance of norms
- ◆ capacity to face discontent and resolve conflict between members.

As educators, we need to put thought into how we group children for certain tasks. We have already mentioned that students perform better with those they like (Masters and Furman, 1981). Sage (2000b) shows how a particular child with SEN functions better in a pair or group of similar ability, because he does not feel threatened by these children. It is important, however, that children have the chance to change groups and learn how to get on with different personalities and abilities. These must be well balanced to avoid less forceful students being dominated.

Some teachers find peer nomination exercises useful in deciding group-work arrangements. This approach was developed by Moreno (1934) and requires children to nominate classmates according to criteria such as 'best friend', 'someone I can work with', and so on. Forced choice group preference records (Frederickson and Graham, 1999) are another possibility, where children are given a questionnaire, similar to the one on the opposite page, and asked to indicate by circling the appropriate face how happy they are to work with certain children.

How much do you like to work with others in class?

Mark	☺	☺	☹
Baljit	☺	☺	☹
Emma	☺	☺	☹
Lin Chan	☺	☺	☹
Marie	☺	☺	☹
David	☺	☺	☹

Groups can be successful because children have the opportunity to explain things to others and develop their thinking and communication to support further learning. Working individually often means that tasks become *practice* rather than *incremental*.

The value of finding out what students think of tasks, and what support they need to complete them, is important. Simpson (1997) suggests a partnership model, in which learning goals are agreed between teachers and students and assessment is shared and formative. I remember using this approach very successfully when teaching English in a secondary school. The students settled on a homework which involved learning a poem and performing it in the next lesson. They devised a sheet to help them identify communication aspects within each student's performance, and the mark each student was awarded was the mean of *everyone's* assessment using the agreed criteria. I have never seen such involved students. There was no messing about in this lesson and they approached the task seriously. I was surprised! It was a 'do or die' situation for me, as many of these 14-year-old students could not write much more than their name, so I decided to develop their ideas through talk, which was an unfamiliar experience in class. This taught me a lesson. Students cannot write before they are able to generate, express and organize their ideas clearly and coherently in speech. You would be surprised how many students have problems with these narrative skills when you test them on retelling tasks (Sage, 2000a). Playground chat deceives. It is mundane without the demands of formal explanations, reports and instructions that entail putting a set of ideas together.

TIP: Try making some joint decisions about tasks with students and encourage them to mark each other's performance to an agreed set of criteria in oral as well as written tasks, as in the example above. (This strategy works well in primary as well as secondary schools – five-year-old children have managed it very successfully.)

Skills for working with others

It is all very well advocating group-work, but do students have the skills to carry it out? Here is a checklist of questions to assess group suitability.

- ◆ **Relationship skills**: Is the child sociable, sympathetic and supportive to others?

- ◆ **Communication skills**: Can the child question, clarify, explain and give and receive instructions confidently?

- ◆ **Assertion skills**: Can the child exercise appropriate independence and assertion?

- ◆ **Conforming skills**: Can the child follow rules and expectations and share happily?

- ◆ **Self-management skills**: Can the child control impulses, show restraint, accept limits or criticisms and reach compromises?

- ◆ **Academic skills**: Can the child produce satisfactory work independently?

TIP: A teaching assistant could assess students' group skills, to assist planning.

There are many students, in primary and secondary schools, who do not match up to these criteria. They are unlikely to learn such skills spontaneously and would benefit from a setting such as a Communication Opportunity Group Scheme (Sage, 2000a), circle time (Mosley, 1996) or nurture group (Boxall, 1996) in which to focus on the specific development of these abilities. A Critical Skills Programme, *Education By Design* (Mobilia and co-workers, 2001), helps teachers to design environments that focus less on teaching and more on learning. Brief information about these schemes is available in Appendix 1 (page 124). The sections that follow also suggest ways in which skills for working with others can be developed.

Supporting

Researchers have identified three useful strategies that can be generally employed by adults to support children in their learning.

- ◆ **Reinforcement** uses praise or other rewards when a child engages in the targeted behaviour, such as asking a question to clarify something.

- ◆ **Shaping** involves rewarding a child, in step-by-step fashion, for increasingly accurate approximations towards the target behaviour, such as an answer to a question. The first step might be an answer to a direct question such as 'What is the monsoon?' This is easier to answer than a clarification question such as 'How does the monsoon operate?' The reason for this is that the first is a closed question, which does not demand a narrative thinking response, putting events together for coherent meaning, as expected in the second, open model.

- ◆ **Modelling** provides a student with a step-by-step demonstration of the components required. This might involve the adult 'thinking aloud' while doing the activity. Pairing students with others who already have the skills provides a natural modelling situation for playing or working with others, resisting aggression or engaging in conversation. The target student is primed to observe the peer model and note what he does.

Coaching

Whereas modelling shows the student what to do, coaching involves telling her in a step-by-step manner. Here is an example of a child being coached to give instructions more successfully.

Step 1   **Introduce the concept**. For example, 'Emma, I want to talk about ideas that make it easier for us to tell others what to do. Let's think and talk about instructions.'

Step 2   **Elicit the child's understanding of the concept**. 'Do you know what giving instructions means? Give me examples.' (For example, ask for instructions on how to sharpen a pencil.)

Step 3   **Analysing the activity**. Repeat the instructions (for sharpening a pencil) and highlight the steps:

1. First, find a pencil sharpener that fits the pencil.
2. Then, place the pencil gently into the hole in the sharpener.
3. After this, turn the pencil carefully in a clockwise direction.
4. Check by removing the pencil to see whether a sharp point has been cut.
5. If the pencil needs more sharpening, replace it in the hole and repeat the turning.
6. When the pencil is sharp enough, remove it from the hole and empty the wood shavings into a waste bin.

Such a simple activity has six definite steps to it and is much more complex than one would imagine! It entails being able to understand the overall goal and locate the stages towards this as well as narrate the activity as a whole idea, using time markers such as 'first', 'then', 'after', 'check', and so on, to link and cohere the information. Critical (left-brain) and creative (right-brain) thinking processes are involved, demonstrating the importance of using both sides of the brain.

Step 4   **Introduce counter examples**. 'Can you give me examples of talk that are not about giving instructions?' (For example, asking questions to find something out, telling a story.) 'What are some of the similarities and differences?'

Step 5   **Trial and Review**. Set up some pair activities where partners give instructions to each other. Ask listeners to feed back whether these were clear and easily followed. Consider together what makes instructions effective. (For example, they give clear steps, don't assume knowledge, are simple to follow and provide full information.)

TIP: Coaching is a role frequently carried out by teaching assistants. Use the framework above to devise a coaching scheme for a child who needs it. Become aware of the narrative thinking and expressive structure skills involved in a task such as giving instructions.

Problem solving

There are several steps to problem solving that are generally evident in programmes using discussions, games and role plays to develop thinking:

1 identification and definition of the problem

2 setting the goal

3 generating alternative solutions

4 considering consequences

5 making a decision on action

6 developing a plan

7 reviewing and evaluating for success.

TIP: This is just the kind of support appreciated by children with high-level logical–mathematic skills (see page 33). Provide them with this guide to work through a problem task.

Foster and co-workers (1996) challenge the idea that social behaviours can be identified independently of the cultural context in which a student interacts. They highlight the problems of working with diverse groups having different attitudes and views. It is important, therefore, for the teacher to remain non-judgemental, accepting all alternative solutions suggested and allowing evaluation from the rest of the class. If the teacher expresses disapproval the discussion is likely to close down.

For example, if the group are discussing the problem of 'Mark bullying Tom', they may suggest beating up Mark as one possible solution to the problem. It is vital to respond neutrally to this idea and support the class in evaluating the consequences of this action. In my experience, children are able to identify more negative consequences of beating someone up than I am, as they are more used to doing it and know what it feels like!

Some will be confused by such discussion because at home they have been encouraged to give as good as they get and behave in macho ways in these circumstances. The teacher's role, here, is to identify other macho ways of dealing with the problem, which have better consequences than bullying. Although schools have rules and sanctions against bullying, inconsistent application by staff is the norm, so creating a student view that they can get away with this sort of behaviour (Sage, 2000b).

TIP: Develop a 'circle time' approach to give opportunities for students to solve their social problems by hearing a range of solutions from others in the group. Running such a group is an appropriate role for a teaching assistant or a learning mentor.

Erwin (1994) examined 43 studies that evaluated the effectiveness of modelling, coaching and problem solving in improving social behaviour of children in class. He concluded that significant improvements were made in their interrelations and thinking abilities. Furnham and Argyle (1981) identified the inability to transfer these skills to other contexts as the 'Achilles heel' of teaching and reported 'a sizeable and largely depressing literature' on the subject. The studies that Furnham and Argyle looked at were clinical in implementation, with children being taught away from the class and having little control of the content; this may be a reason for the lack of transfer, along with differences in the structure of the settings.

Programmes that give attention to thinking, communication and the social context are found to work best in improving children's ability to work together, as they consider a broader range of skills with a wider application beyond the classroom (Sage, 2000b). Teaching skills that are valued in everyday settings become naturally reinforced when they occur there. The Communication Opportunity Group Scheme (Sage, 2000a), the 'circle of friends' approach (Mosley, 1996) and nurture groups (Boxall, 1996) are interventions that involve peers in helping to change one another's behaviour for the better and have the potential to alter children's attitudes and responses to each other. This provides a link that is missing in the studies reviewed by Furnham and Argyle.

TIP: If you do not know about the schemes mentioned above, find out about them! Their implementation can make a big impact on standards. Read brief summaries of them in Appendix 1 (page 124).

Cartledge and Milburn (1996) review evidence that co-operative classroom learning activities contribute to positive peer interactions and acceptance of SEN and racial differences, as well as academic achievement. They suggest this approach is particularly relevant for African, Asian and Hispanic Americans, whose cultural roots are in collectivist rather than individualistic societies.

Comment

Considering personality differences is vital for co-operative learning activities that play a major part in school life. There are thousands of possible combinations of characteristics that make up our person. We might be jolly, easy-going, determined, optimistic, shy, quiet, hardworking, anxious or volatile, but whatever our dispositions, personality has a profound effect on all our behaviour, including our learning and achievement. Educators need to be aware of personality differences that might clash and disrupt the successful functioning of groups. While it is possible to ameliorate antisocial characteristics, it is not easy to change our basic natures, which arrive with us at birth.

◆ Intelligence

Anyone is only as good as their hands.

A traditional saying

Now we enter a battlefield! The word 'intelligence' is a convenient term to overview a person's mental abilities but has provoked much debate and dissension. It is traditionally summarized as an intelligence quotient (IQ), obtained from a scale that includes a variety of verbal and non-verbal tests. Today, these are largely discredited but their influence lingers on, especially in educational circles.

IQ testing

So what does IQ testing comprise?

- ◆ a range of mentally challenging tasks
- ◆ a standard presentation of tasks
- ◆ results compared with norms from a representative sample

The use of a norm-based instrument to identify and differentiate children has been controversial. Those in favour emphasize that IQs:

- ◆ provide an estimate of mental potential
- ◆ draw on comparison data
- ◆ screen for information processing problems
- ◆ provide a baseline against which to measure future development.

Critics produce counter-arguments:

- ◆ IQs are less reliable than claimed
- ◆ norm-based tests are valid only for the standardized populations
- ◆ IQs do not give useful information for teaching
- ◆ a number score gives misleading scientific precision as tests measure only a narrow range of abilities.

What is intelligence?

It is not clear what is meant by intelligence. Here are three early definitions:

1 ability to think in abstract ways (Terman, 1925)

2 global capacity to think rationally, act purposefully and deal effectively with the environment (Wechsler, 1944)

3 innate, general thinking ability (Burt, 1957).

Each of these pioneers was influenced by the purposes for which he was using the term and the ideas of the times. This has resulted in subtly different concepts. Terman identified the mental capacities of gifted people, while Wechsler guided damaged war veterans towards independence and Burt advised on educational selection procedures.

Terman questioned the basis for designating some kinds of mental activity as higher than others. Why should someone who finds abstractions difficult but handles tools skilfully be deemed less intelligent than a person who writes poetry and solves mathematical puzzles? Individuals differ in having different *kinds* of intelligence.

Two developments have supported this view of human diversity. The first is the recognition that there are cultural differences in what is deemed intelligent. For example, speed of response is more highly valued in some societies than others and the context in which a task is presented affects performance, depending on cultural familiarity (Ceci, 1996). The second has been the introduction of a theory of multiple intelligences (Gardner, 1993a). This approach puts less emphasis on the correlation of mental abilities, suggesting a general factor of intelligence. More attention is given to the fact that they do not correlate perfectly, proposing distinct abilities.

Gardner's definition takes a wider view of intelligence, highlighting ability to solve problems or create products that are valued within one or more cultural settings. Academic and practical abilities are, thus, both acknowledged. Intelligence defines an ability for which there is evidence that it develops separately in some way. An example of such evidence is brain damage resulting in the loss of a particular ability while others are retained. Examples of the intelligences Gardner had in mind include:

- **linguistic** – speaking, listening (understanding), reading and writing

- **logical–mathematic** – logical reasoning and mathematics problem solving

- **musical** – appreciating music structure and playing an instrument

- **bodily-kinesthetic** – gesturing, dancing, running, playing and constructing

- **interpersonal** – relating to and understanding others' feelings and behaviour

- **intrapersonal** – understanding oneself and how to change.

33

TASK: Play a game with your class. Write brief definitions of each intelligence on large cards and place them in a line on the floor. Get students to stand in front of the one that they think best describes them. Do some feel they fit more than one category? Compile a bar chart to look at the class distribution. Discuss how you can use information about people's intelligences to help learning (see list below).

Gardner stresses that this is not a definitive list and what we observe as intelligent behaviour is usually the result of an interaction of intelligences. He suggests (1993b) that these ideas could be the basis for an approach to the school curriculum that takes account of individual differences, allowing students different *entry points*. Teachers, therefore, need to provide various forms of stimulation and experience to meet the needs of children with a wide range of intelligences, in the following way.

1 **Linguistic**: give opportunities for talk.

2 **Logical–mathematic**: provide step-by-step approaches to tasks (flow diagrams).

3 **Musical**: allow personal stereos if music helps students work; use jingles to learn facts.

4 **Bodily-kinesthetic**: give opportunities for role play, drama and other active learning.

5 **Interpersonal**: give opportunities for group-working and discussion.

6 **Intrapersonal**: give personal space and chances to work alone (individual action plan).

TASK: List these learning methods on a worksheet and ask students to rank them for preference. For example, a student might rank number 4 (bodily-kinesthetic) as the most preferred method and method 6 (intrapersonal) as the least. Develop a bar chart of class preferences and work out, for each of the six methods, the percentage of students giving it the top rank.

Comment

Teachers have always intuitively recognized the different intelligences or abilities of students and used their strengths to facilitate other learning. For example, musical ability has been used to learn number tables, through songs, on the basis that most children are competent with sound rhythms and can use these as a structure on which to map new sequences. The descriptions of intelligences above can be employed to rank our abilities and use the better ones to facilitate weaker areas. For example, if a child is good at interpersonal skills but weak at logical–mathematic ones, pair him up with a student having an opposite strength and then they can learn from one another.

TIP: Pair up children with complementary patterns of strengths and weaknesses, so that they have the opportunity to learn strategies from each other.

My experience is that able children have good measures of all intelligences, which supports Gardner's view that intelligent behaviour is an interaction between them. On the other hand, there are those who excel in one area, but are unable to make the best of that skill because of weaknesses in other areas. I know a young man, for example, who is an outstanding cricketer and gifted in bodily-kinesthetic intelligence. Nevertheless, he is shy and indifferent in his approach to life, with such low inter- and intrapersonal skills that he barely communicates, so it is unlikely that he will make the higher echelons of his sport. Communicating is the best way to reach the top because by clarifying issues and discussing with others you gain information for building further skills. You miss out terribly on those fine points of learning that make you outstanding if you do not communicate effectively. Communication is also essential in dealing with the media and presenting oneself positively, confidently and co-operatively. Lacking this skill will seriously impede development of any type. Performance thus depends on the integration of physical, mental, emotional and social abilities and the influence of basic personality features on these.

Learning styles and strategies

Discussion about individual intelligence has focused on claims that it is genetically determined and cannot be modified. Jenson (1969), a proponent of this view, suggested two levels of intelligence and a teaching approach that taught to a child's particular abilities.

- ◆ **Association and reproduction**: as in learning a series such as days of the week.

- ◆ **Transformation and abstraction**: as in learning new concepts or solving a problem where the answer is not clear.

Opponents of this view argued that ability is modifiable if individuals are given appropriate strategies and support. Genetic factors produce variations in the *level of responsiveness* and require corresponding variations in the quality and quantity of learning input (Feuerstein, 1979). There is no fixed limit to learning, provided that it is suitably facilitated.

Sternberg's triarchic theory of intelligence (1985) describes how the human mind deals with the external world. It defines two basic abilities:

- ◆ the ability to automate the processing of information

- ◆ the ability to deal with new tasks.

For example, children cannot read fluently unless they can both process letter shapes without conscious attention and also analyse new words. In contrast to most theorists, Sternberg was interested in the three mental processes through which intelligence operates, shown in the table overleaf.

Type of process	Aim	Activities
Analytic	Solve problems by manipulating elements/relationships	Comparing, Analysing, Evaluating
Creative	Solve new problems by thinking in novel ways about the problem and its elements	Creating, Inventing, Designing
Practical	Solve problems by applying everyday knowledge	Applying, Using, Implementing

TASK: Using the triarchic model as a guide, work out which processes are developed or under-developed in a particular child. This is an assessment task that can be carried out by a teaching assistant.

Use this analysis to encourage an incremental approach to building up students' abilities. It is logical that comparing knowledge is easier than inventing a new way to solve problems. Bloom's taxonomy of educational objectives (1956) is based on this hierarchical approach, and is discussed on page 73. In many tasks, students need all three mental processes, but the model is useful in identifying a variety of elements and giving us a framework for observing which are developed in individual students. It allows us to be judicious in the tasks we set and helps us avoid giving children problems that are either too easy or too difficult to solve.

Our ability to undertake a task and complete it requires intelligence but also attention, motivation, determination and persistence. These are personality features, as already described, and may be encouraged or tempered if not completely changed. It has been shown, moreover, that children who do not generally succeed with academic tasks can be taught more effective learning strategies, particularly in the way they remember things (Male, 1996; Sage, 2003).

A person's learning style is their characteristic way of assimilating and processing information (Cameron and Reynolds, 1999). Individual learning style may be as important as differences in ability. There are three key dimensions to the way a person approaches the task of dealing with information:

 processing

 organizing

 representing.

Processing

Information is processed through five senses: hearing, sight, feeling/touch, smell and taste. Academic learning involves mainly the first three channels and research suggests we have a preference for one type of input, even though we integrate information from all routes for overall meaning. Smith (1998) presented evidence to suggest the following distribution of learning preferences in the human population.

Channel	Percentage of population preferring to learn using this input channel (%)
Kinesthetic (movement/touch – called the Haptic channel by medical personnel)	37
Auditory (hearing)	34
Visual	29

TASK: Try the simple information processing quiz in Appendix 2 (page 128) on yourself and your class. You will find some people who do not have a clear learning preference but most will. Discuss what you could do with this information. (For example, you might try sitting those with an auditory preference in the front, the 'visuals' in the middle, and the 'kinesthetics' at the back with things to fiddle with, as they need to be active.) Make a class bar chart to compare information processing preferences.

So, there may be a roughly equal distribution of learning preferences within a class. It is worth remembering that we tend to teach emphasizing our own preferred method of processing. This means if that if you have an auditory preference you are likely to do a great deal of talking, so beware!

It is a fact that in classrooms we give less and less opportunity for active learning, even though kinesthetic processing is the preferred method in distribution terms. Subjects that used to be practical have become totally academic. I observed a food technology lesson for a term and was looking forward to tasting scones and shepherd's pie. No such luck, I'm afraid, as the children did no cooking. Instead, they learned the theory behind nutrition, and planned meals for old ladies with strokes, nursing mothers and sick infants, for example. A practical subject had been turned on its head, because of today's stringent health and safety rules. How can we make our lessons more hands-on to suit the bulk of our learners? Although active experiences might take more effort to plan and set up, rewards are reaped in terms of increased understanding and involvement of learners. Such experiences suit boys, in particular, who need more energetic outlets to cope with physical growth demands.

Organizing

There is support for the theory that we tend to organize information in wholes and parts. Miller (1984) presented a visual puzzle to subjects and found they tried to solve it first by either looking for an overall shape ('top-down' method) or building up individual parts ('bottom-up' method). Look at the puzzle below. What do you make of it? What strategy did you use? Did you try the second strategy if the first did not work for you? Check Appendix 3 (page 130) for the solution.

TASK: Try out Miller's puzzle. Do you prefer to work as a 'top-down' or a 'bottom-up' organizer? Try this out with colleagues and students.

Miller used this analysis to look at students with reading problems and suggested they lacked one of these organizing strategies, particularly the top-down one. This is confirmed by my own experience of children with learning difficulties. These students normally lack the ability to organize the whole meaning of something. This greatly impairs their capacity to understand talk and text, which depends on the bottom-up process of building up sounds and the top-down process of building meaning from sentence information. Such construction involves reference, inference and coherence skills and the result is known as narrative structure, which pulls together a series of events to make a whole entity.

TASK: Can you work out the reference, inference and coherence strategies in this text?

'Luke and Borage were sitting on the grass. Suddenly, Borage raced off after a cat, which was slinking in the bushes. At the same time, he was closely pursued by his master, who managed to catch him and put a lead on his collar. They continued walking. After a while, dark clouds threatened. Soon, they broke into a run to reach home quickly.'

	Examples in the text (see 'Task' at bottom of page 38)
References new words referring to established things/events	*which* (the cat) *he* (Borage) *his* (Borage), *master* (Luke), *him* (Borage), *his* (Borage) *they* (Borage and Luke)
Inferences clues available in the content	*sitting on the grass* (weather is fine and warm and the couple are outside) *Luke* (is a male – clue: name) *Borage* (is a dog – clue: name, collar and lead) *pursued* (dog might torment/injure the cat unless he is caught and put on the lead) *master* (Luke owns Borage) *dark clouds* (going to rain) *broke into a run* (rain has started, and the dog and his master want to avoid getting wet) *home* (Luke and Borage live together).
Coherences word/phrase time markers that signal changes in events	*suddenly* (marks time shift) *at the same time* (signifies simultaneous action) *after a while* (signals a time period and a change in circumstances) *soon* (indicates an alteration in events).

Analysis of narrative structure, such as the example above, demonstrates the complexity of putting together meaning for understanding either talk or text. Bell (1991) provides case study information about this organizing problem. This supports the view that most students with learning difficulties do not have a top-down strategy, but if it is intact their outlines lack detail – instead of getting a clear 'big picture', these students get only a very rough sketch. Subjects employing both strategies, however, are able to assemble a deeper level of meaning. Miller suggests that here, again, we have a *preferred strategy* and the population distribution for this is roughly 50:50. Now I understand why, when I was a child, I could complete a jigsaw puzzle without the box-lid picture (bottom-up preferred strategy), whereas my sister needed that picture to grasp the meaning of the relationship between the pieces (top-down preferred strategy).

I experienced another demonstration of this dichotomy of organizational strategies when I worked at Central School of Speech and Drama and had the privilege of observing Jonathan Miller taking Master Classes for post-graduate students. He originally trained as a neurologist and then moved into the Arts world. Perching on the edge of the stage, he talked, in conversational style, about the relationships between scientific knowledge of the body and artistic performance. After the session, I was sure that half the audience must have thought him wonderful, while the other half had probably failed to understand his message. This was because he presented information in typical bottom-up style, with no overview or steps towards the goal.

As a bottom-up processor myself, I thought Jonathan was wonderful. As Miller's research (1984) indicated, we learn best with those who have the same information organizing style as ourselves. But of course this has implications for those who do not have the same organizing style as the teacher. Knowing your own preferred organizing style, as a teacher, will help you to adjust your communication structure to suit the whole class. This means presenting a clear overview (sometimes called an advance organizer) and steps towards the goal for those who have a top-down preference, and giving detail and illustrative anecdotes for those who prefer a data-driven, bottom-up style. I know I am a conversational performer who finds it difficult to give overviews and signposts to the eventual goal of my presentation. If I am to reach both halves of my audience, however, I must be sure to include such organizational aids to accommodate the needs of those whose processing preference is complementary to my own.

TIP: Make a point of writing on the board a two- or three-line summary of each lesson, and steps towards the goal, so that students can remind themselves of the aim and plan. Don't forget to include plenty of details and anecdotes in your presentation!

Representing

This dimension considers how we represent information in words and pictures during thinking.

Imagine giving me directions to the nearest shop from your house. How did you do it? Did you visualize the route? You probably did, otherwise it would have been difficult to direct me successfully. Now, tell me on which side is the hot tap on your bathroom washbasin? Did you visualize your bathroom to give me the correct answer? It would be well nigh impossible to be right if you were unable to represent the information visually.

Let's try another trick. Can you think of a white flower on a black background? Are you able to make a picture of this in your mind? My image was of a clump of snowdrops, in the dark earth, under a sycamore tree outside my kitchen window. What was yours? A lily on black velvet? A daisy on black paper? A rose on the lapel of a dark suit? It was probably different from my representation, which demonstrates the difficulty of communicating ideas!

Bell (1991) has spent a career looking at visualizing and verbalizing. Although Bell acknowledges that we might have a preference for representing ideas in words or in pictures, she stresses the importance of being able to visualize from both spoken and written information. She presents evidence suggesting that those who are weak visualizers have problems in understanding talk and text. Interviews with subjects demonstrate that those with excellent comprehension skills are able to create 'movies in their heads' and see what they are processing from words heard or seen.

These ideas are akin to the Greek mnemonic strategies, by which one builds memories of information using picture links. They are described in detail in *Lend Us Your Ears* (Sage, 2003), which looks at how we comprehend the great welter of narrative information that we are faced with in classes today.

Bell's evidence is important because there are countless studies (cited by Bell, 1991, and Sage, 2003) which show that children with learning difficulties experience problems in visualizing information. This has serious consequences for learning as they fail to comprehend talk and text accurately. Bell and Sage suggest strategies to help remedy this difficulty and it is worth consulting these books if you really want to understand how we comprehend.

Below are some tips to help develop the visualizing process. Regular practice at visualizing need only take a minute but is invaluable in building this representative function for thinking, problem solving and understanding.

TIP: At the start of a lesson, ask students to close their eyes for 30 seconds (the average time it takes to make a picture in your mind) and visualize an object or person that is part of the lesson. For example, if the topic is about mammals, suggest that students think of a mammal that they know (dog, cat, cow, horse and so on) and picture this in their minds before describing it to a partner.

Try to create opportunities in lessons when students have to visualize a character in a story, or a place that is being talked about, for example.

Riding and Rayner (1998) provide a 'cognitive control' model that integrates the sensory input, wholist–analytic and verbal–imager dimensions. They suggest that a person's memory of past experiences plays a significant role in the development of their characteristic learning style. As might be expected, there is much evidence of cultural differences in learning styles (Hickson and co-workers 1994; Anderson, 1995).

It is not clear what implications theories of information processing, organizing and representing have for teaching methods. Research has generally yielded inconsistent results, when attempts have been made to evaluate the impact of matching teaching methods to students' assessed learning styles (McKenna, 1990). Initial results, using a questionnaire based on the cognitive control model that integrates processes, have been more promising (Riding and Rayner, 1998).

In the educational world these ideas are relatively novel, but in the medical profession, they have long been in fashion in diagnostic assessment and intervention. The Illinois Test of Psycholinguistic Abilities (McCarthy and Kirk, 1961) is one example of the assessment of learning styles with a view to intervention. Although popular in the 1960s with speech and language therapists, it has lost favour in an increasingly pressured world, because of the complexity of the assessment and teaching techniques. There is clear evidence of its efficacy, however, in clinical contexts.

Emotional intelligence

The role of 'affect' or 'emotion' has often been overlooked in educational practice. There has been increasing interest in recent years, however, in 'emotional intelligence' and the part it plays in learning. The concept was introduced by Salovey and Mayer (1990) and popularized by Goleman (1996), who defined five dimensions:

◆ knowing one's emotions

◆ managing emotions

◆ motivating oneself

◆ recognizing emotions in others

◆ handling relationships.

There is considerable overlap between these five domains and social skills. Critics suggest that the concept of emotional intelligence adds little to our knowledge. Salovey and Sluyter (1997) revised their definition of the term in response to this criticism:

> Emotional intelligence involves the ability to perceive accurately, appraise and express emotion; the ability to access and/or generate feelings when they facilitate thought; the ability to understand emotion and emotional knowledge; the ability to regulate emotions to promote emotional and intellectual growth.

These ideas emphasize emotional contributions to intelligence, separating them from social abilities and personal dispositions included in earlier definitions. They are elaborated in a multidimensional, developmental model summarized in the table below.

Emotional Intelligence: A summary of Salovey and Sluyter's definition (1997)				
Area of definition	Level 1	Level 2	Level 3	Level 4
Regulating emotions	Open to emotions	Detach from emotion	Reflect on emotions	Manage emotions
Understanding and analysing emotions	Label emotions	Interpret emotions	Complex emotions	Emotion transitions
Emotions facilitating thinking	Prioritize thinking	Aid judgement and memory	Encourage views	Facilitate solutions
Evaluating and expressing emotion	Identify own	Identify others	Express accurately	Discriminate

The model has not been fully tested and applied to help children's emotional development. Research based on other developmental frameworks (for example, Piaget, 1964) shows an overlap between levels or stages, and this is likely to be the case here. Nevertheless, the theory provides a structure for discussion and reflection, raising the profile of emotions in social and academic development.

Teaching awareness of emotions

Greenberg and co-workers (1995) evaluated the PATHS programme (Promoting Alternative Thinking Strategies). The 35-lesson unit on Feelings and Relationships focuses on emotional and interpersonal understanding. Students were taught that all feelings were acceptable but all behaviours were not. They were asked to attend to what their feelings were telling them and use this information to decide what to do next. Labelling feelings was seen as an important basis for helping self-control and solving problems successfully. There was instruction in using cues and recognizing feelings in oneself and others, managing them and deciding whether to show or hide what is felt. In addition, children were helped to understand the effect of their behaviour on others. The study found the programme effective for both mainstream and special needs students in Years 3 and 4, in:

◆ improving vocabulary and fluency in discussing emotional experiences

◆ enhancing belief in ability to manage emotions

◆ developing understanding of the various aspects of emotion.

The programme and evaluation addressed only two of Salovey and Sluyter's four dimensions of emotional intelligence, but presents a step forward and suggests the benefits of highlighting emotional issues in educational experiences.

TIP: Try creating a 'wall of feelings'. Give each child a rectangle-shaped piece of paper. Ask them all to draw or write how they are feeling at present. Pin responses on the wall and analyse predominant feelings under various criteria – happy / sad; energetic / tired, and so on. Which is the most common feeling? Do this every day for a week and see how feelings change. Explore why.

◆ The role of motivation in learning

We cannot leave the discussion regarding personality and intelligence in learning without considering how motivation influences these aspects. Three main theories are worthy of reflection:

 Self-determination (Deci and Ryan, 1985). This theory considers the ideas of extrinsic motivation (rewards from outside yourself) and intrinsic motivation (rewards from inside yourself). There is a continuum from no motivation to intrinsic motivation, arising from a strong personal wish to achieve something. Issues in this theory are competition, relationships to others and autonomy.

43

2 **Goal achievement** (Nicholls, 1991). Ideas centre on the process rather than the product of the motivation.

3 **Need achievement** (Atkinson, 1974). This view suggests that we are motivated either to approach success or to avoid failure. Wentzel (1991) stressed *social goals* as an important motivational factor and considered the multidimensional nature of these.

Motivation, as suggested by these three main approaches, is a complex issue that involves inherited personality features. It is influenced by intelligence and the interest and support of our parents or carers, as well as opportunities to develop our potential in ways that are congenial to us. Since it is an essential factor in personal and academic success, we need to consider what helps or hinders the motivation of our students. One thing is certain – we are all driven by different things. The fact that my father promised me a brand new bike if I passed my eleven-plus examination was not in the least bit motivating for me, as a reluctant cyclist. A holiday in Iceland would have been much more enticing (though a somewhat extravagant incentive for an eleven year old, I admit!).

◆ Review

Personality has great impact on potential and performance and, although it is not possible to change someone's basic make-up, unhelpful characteristics can be tempered to improve learning. COGS, circle time or nurture groups are useful formats to help students use their attributes positively. As school is a group experience, a blend of personalities is necessary to make it work. There are negatives as well as positives for working in groups and it is important to be aware of the purpose of an experience so that students can be placed appropriately. There will be class members who do not have group skills – these can be assessed and worked on using reinforcing, shaping and modelling strategies, which research suggests are successful. Educators need to become aware of what makes groups effective and seek to achieve good dynamics among members.

Intelligence integrates with personality as the base for learning but it is a controversial concept. Although it was conceived originally to define academic processes, recent theories have broadened to consider practical abilities as well. Related to the mental activities of thinking and problem solving are our particular processing, organizing and representing styles of learning. Although new ideas in education, they have been in use in therapeutic circles for many years and shown to have utility and validity. A greater application of them in schools will provide classroom evidence to compare with clinical data.

More recently, we have added the concept of emotional intelligence to the learning debate. Since all information input is filtered through our feelings first, this domain points to the importance of a nurturing environment, which fosters our emotional state as a requisite to learning. Motivation to learn is influenced by personality and intelligence but also strongly by environmental factors, which develop or dim our desires to achieve. The skill is finding out what helps or hinders this process. We need to become aware of the very different things that inspire us to achieve.

MAIN POINTS

◆ Personality characteristics are present at birth but can be moulded to assist learning.

◆ Children have to learn to blend their personality with others in different groups and may need to acquire skills to help them interrelate well.

◆ Groups have positive and negative aspects and educators need to be clear about the attributes of a successful one.

◆ Children can learn group skills in specific learning schemes and have these generally facilitated through reinforcement, shaping and modelling strategies.

◆ Intelligence integrates with personality features to realize learning potential using practical, analytic and creative abilities.

◆ Information processing, organizing and representing styles are as important as basic intelligence in mastering learning.

◆ Information filters first through our feelings so emotional intelligence is likely to have a major impact on performance and requires a nurturing environment.

◆ Motivation has intrinsic and extrinsic aspects that influence our will to succeed and will be different for each one of us because of our basic differences.

Chapter Three

What are social class, gender and race differences?

Overview

Social class, gender and race differences are considered together since there are obvious links between them in the school context. Children's backgrounds must be considered when presenting information to them, so that it is relevant and meaningful to their lives. This chapter introduces practical issues that continually challenge educators. Every attempt is made to provide useful suggestions that can be tried in schools.

◆ Social class

Social classes are evident in most societies and are a way of categorizing people according to their occupation and economic level. Therefore, those who have high levels of professional training and expertise will be at the top level of the Registrar General's social class classification whereas the completely unskilled will find themselves at the bottom. Such groupings are divisive and, in a society that values equality, our status should depend on meritocracy rather than class position. Policies of inclusion and more open access to higher education are helping to provide more opportunities for a wider range of the population, but the cost of these will a barrier to many.

In spite of attempts to open up opportunities, the instability of modern lives, due to changing family patterns and job insecurity, has produced a sizeable underclass in this country. There are an increasing number of lone parents, many of whom find it difficult to get and keep jobs because of their family responsibilities (Beresford, 1995). In inner cities, particularly, there are ghettos of poverty, though there are areas of economic deprivation in rural populations too.

Children from socially and economically deprived backgrounds start school with grave disadvantages. They will be less well-nourished and healthy and likely to lack life experiences that are essential for mental, emotional and social growth. I have met children living in a Birmingham housing estate who, incredibly, have never been to the city centre a mile away.

These children have also never seen fields and cows, except on television; they have no real understanding of the countryside because they have not visited and experienced it.

These issues are disturbing because children excluded from school are more likely to have experienced poverty, homelessness, parental illness and bereavement (Ofsted, 1996; Hayden, 1997). Disproportionate numbers of children who are looked after by local authorities have been excluded and come from lower social classes (Brodie and Berridge, 1996). Research shows that a larger proportion of those from disadvantaged groups have special educational needs as a consequence of their socio-economic conditions. For example, these children are more likely to develop diseases such as measles, pneumonia and tuberculosis and develop secondary cerebral infections leading to disability such as deafness (Molteno and co-workers, 1990; Donald, 1994).

Thus, environmental factors may influence development in a range of different ways. These can be analysed using the following criteria commonly employed in clinical diagnosis (Sage, 1998):

◆ **predisposing factors**, which create a situation favourable to the behaviour development

◆ **precipitating factors**, which initially trigger the behaviour

◆ **perpetuating factors**, which encourage the behaviour to persist.

In the example below, these criteria are used in conjunction with child, family, school and community dimensions to plot a child with communication difficulties.

An analysis of a five-year-old boy's communication difficulties				
Factors	**Child**	**Family**	**School**	**Community**
Predisposing	Measles, deafness, slow talking, shy No play/nursery experiences	Lone mother (asthmatic) with dysfluency No siblings	No speech and language support available	Family isolated and marginalized – no close family/friends
Precipitating	Stressed by new group communication demands	No preparation made for school. Mum has not kept speech and language therapy appointments	Many group activities – child does not have the skills to join in	No opportunities to belong to after-school groups
Perpetuating	Anxious and not willing to take risks with talking in school	Reactions from Mum reinforce poor communication	Child has no legal statement so no guaranteed support	Contacts outside school reinforce problem by talking for the child

This approach helps us understand the wide range of factors involved, but where do we start in trying to put this child's life right and building his base to support learning? There are decisions to be made. First, what needs to be done? Second, who needs to do it?

What needs to be done?	Who needs to do it?
Assess communication abilities in one-to-one and group contexts. Devise plan to meet assessed needs and make it known to all relevant staff so they can support when appropriate.	Teaching assistant/SENCO and a speech and language therapist if possible.
Assess teaching approaches and group arrangements to see if these are preventing the development of communication in school.	Teacher in conjunction with teaching assistant involved in the class activities.
Talk with the child to see how he feels about school and the support he needs.	Adult who best relates to the child: teacher/teaching assistant, learning mentor, SENCO or other.
Talk with Mum to explain school difficulties and gain her view on how to support at home. Encourage her to look at the support she needs and how she can best achieve it.	Adult who best relates to the Mum (as above).
Enlist peer support in circle time, COGS or nurture group to ensure that the child is not dominated and has the chance to use communication at his level and be stimulated to relate to others.	Teaching assistant, learning mentor or other appropriate adult who is trained to take the group.

This analysis only takes a few minutes but locates the range of factors that must to be addressed in helping children succeed.

TASK: Use the framework above to look at a child you know. What are the things most easily put right and which need a great deal of attention?

Do you have an overwhelming feeling that children with barriers to learning are always going to struggle in mainstream settings? Perhaps this is the reason that so many of them find themselves eventually in special schools for children with moderate learning difficulties. The social profile of these schools has shown a high proportion of students from lower socio-economic groups and this has remained so over time. It is notable, though, that the over-representation of lower-class children is *not* found in forms of special provision that carry less social stigma, such as classes for children with specific learning difficulties (Riddell and co-workers, 1994). Tomlinson (1988) analysed this situation using 'critical theory':

> Critical theorists of education systems are concerned to map injustices and inequalities. They see a sharp contrast between liberal humanitarian rhetoric that education is a force for good, for progress, and for equality, and the reality that education systems often mirror, or contribute to, an unequal, competitive, uncaring society. They have noted the way in which education often helps to reproduce the children of minorities, the working class, and handicapped children into inferior, powerless social positions. They do not see terms such as 'ability', 'achievement', or 'failure' as objective or disinterested terms, but as social categories, socially constructed by groups who have the power to label others as failures, and they examine processes of labelling and categorisation, as events, which usually serve the vested interests of particular groups.

49

Comment

Most seriously, in England, the national curriculum accentuates class differences. The introduction of standard age-related tests means that children are ranked and ordered as never before and their value to school and workplace will vary accordingly. Children are measured against fixed norms, which provide powerful controls. The publishing of test results in league tables has led to the differentiation of student groups. They can become segregated from one another in bands or streams and follow different educational paths and social destinies. This works against equality of opportunity but sits well with the present system of grammar schools, comprehensives, city technology colleges, foundation and independent schools (Lawton, 1999).

◆ Gender

In recent years, there has been a preoccupation with gender issues as girls now outperform boys at all levels of the UK education system. In 2001, 55.4 per cent of girls achieved five or more A*–C grades at GCSE as against 44.5 per cent of boys (Ofsted and Equal Opportunities Commission, 2001). Post-16, 76 per cent of girls stayed on in full-time education or training but only 67 per cent of boys did so. In the 1970s, girls were seen as the underachievers but in 2002, by contrast, 55 per cent of graduates were women, who were awarded more first- and upper second-class degrees than men. Social and economic changes have made women aware of what they can achieve. Schools have made a conscious effort to reverse the underachievement of girls. Now, the balance has tipped the other way.

About 83 per cent of students excluded from school are boys, who are 15 times more likely than girls to be barred from primary school and 4–5 times more likely to be so in secondary settings. The reasons have been much debated. Intellectually, there are no remarkable differences between girls and boys, although girls tend to score higher on verbal tests whereas boys do better at spatial ones. Some brain differences are suggested, as the left-brain serves mostly verbal activities and the right-brain mainly spatial ones. Certainly, school is now a very verbal environment with curriculum demands leading to increasing levels of 'teacher talk' (Hislam, 2002). There are fewer practical activities in classes because of health and safety curbs, so even active subjects such as science and technology have become more academically biased. Such changes have been referred to as a 'feminization' of the curriculum, and this description has credence if we consider physical differences between the sexes.

Physical differences

Until puberty, there are few differences in physical prowess between boys and girls. Adolescence is earlier and shorter for girls, occurring generally between 11 and 14 years of age, and as a result girls have lower average height. At about ten, boys have a large increase in muscle growth and become twice as strong as girls. Their puberty starts at around 13 and finishes at 17 years.

In connection with physical development, we need to consider hormones and their effect on growth and learning potential. Before birth, the hormone androgen determines the child's sexual characteristics. After birth, males and females are essentially equivalent in the amounts of sex hormones in the blood, as far as we can presently test them. At this stage, the growth hormones come into play. The pituitary, thyroid, adrenal and pancreas glands develop before birth and their secretions govern a child's growth throughout development.

The role of hormones in puberty is complex. Rapid physical growth and development of the reproductive systems, as well as secondary sex characteristics, are triggered and maintained by sharp increases in hormone levels. In girls, oestrogen levels increase, and produce the menstrual cycle. In boys, higher levels of testosterone lead to their reproductive systems developing towards maturity.

Sex hormones are themselves triggered by activating hormones released by the pituitary gland and these stimulate a range of growth-related hormones in the body. The range of ages at which these changes occur is large and puberty takes place anytime between 10 and 17 years of age, with heredity and environment playing some part. For example, malnutrition interferes with physical and mental growth.

There is a large body of evidence (Tanner, 1970) suggesting that children who are more rapid in physical growth are also advanced in mental growth. They score higher on intelligence tests and do better in school than more slowly developing peers. This is partly explained by the fact that fast developers acquire an early confidence about themselves and may be treated differently by others. Bee (2000) points out that the largest children are most likely to be leaders.

Researchers have found a relationship between physical maturation and personality. Sheldon (1940) was the first to identify three body types: 'endomorphic' (amount of fat – soft and round); 'mesomorphic' (amount of muscle – squarely built); 'ectomorphic' (length of bone – tall and thin). Endomorphic boys were rated by teachers as assertive and aggressive, the mesomorphs were viewed as leaders and confident and quarrelsome, whereas the ectomorphs were seen as thoughtful, considerate but lacking in energy (Walker, 1962; Cortes and Gatti, 1965). Where do differences in teacher perceptions come from? One possibility is that society as a whole has clear assumptions about people and their body build. We expect muscular children to be athletic but 'thin Jims' to be future professors. The first group might be encouraged in sport while the second propelled towards reading.

Hormones, also, have an effect on personality. Those with high concentrations of the male hormone are likely to be dominant and aggressive. Therefore, by adolescence, the sex differences appear marked, with boys showing twice as much physical strength and aggression as girls. Hormone effects and physical prowess probably exacerbate tough behaviour in males. Consistency in aggression through life is more apparent in males than females. There is reason to suppose that the baby comes equipped with a link between frustration and aggression, as this is such a common response in all children. Other responses to frustration can be learned. Some child-rearing practices have been consistently linked with high levels of aggression and these include rejection and frequent physical punishment. Do boys suffer greater frustration and more physical punishment? What do you think?

Stereotypes

There is some interesting research (Condry and Condry, 1976; Condry and Ross, 1985) suggesting that boys and girls are judged differently in terms of what constitutes aggression. Subjects viewed a videotape of a child responding to a stimulating toy such as a jack-in-the-box. Ratings of the type and intensity of the emotions displayed varied, depending on whether subjects were told the infant was a boy or a girl. Those who thought the child was a boy were likely to rate an ambiguous negative response as anger, whereas if the same child was thought to be a girl, she was viewed as being fearful in the same situation.

In a second study, subjects viewed a videotape of two children playing in the snow and were asked to rate the degree of aggression of one target child. Snowsuits disguised the children's sex and gender labels were varied. Subjects rated the target child as significantly less aggressive if they thought it was a boy with a boy, than if they believed it was a boy or girl with another girl. The effect was particularly strong in those subjects experienced with children, suggesting that they expected higher levels of aggression in play between boys than in other conditions. This led subjects to discount aggressiveness if they thought the children were boys, or to inflate it if they thought they were girls, or both. Gender stereotypes are, therefore, apparent and Hill (1994) has demonstrated these in teacher assessments of students, interpreting the same behaviour differently in a boy and a girl.

Tasks and tests

The format of tasks or tests in school has been found to have a differential impact between sexes. Boys do better on multiple-choice questions while girls are better at essay writing (Wood, 1991; Gipps and Murphy, 1994; Willingham and Cole, 1997). Various explanations have been offered for this. Perhaps girls' essays are evaluated more favourably simply because they are more fluent in their writing and produce longer answers (Pomplun and Capps, 1999). Maybe girls underperform on multiple-choice formats because they appear more likely than boys to omit items when they are unsure of answers. Boys, on the other hand, tend to guess when they are uncertain (Hanna, 1986; Linn and co-workers, 1987). Whatever the explanation, the solution is to provide a mixture of formats and minimize this bias. It is always useful to carry out a feedback exercise to check how students have experienced demands made on them.

TIP: Try to mix up tasks and tests, providing both multiple-choice and essays to minimize sex bias. Check student responses to the experience.

Reading

There are many more boys with reading difficulties than girls (Riddell and co-workers, 1994). It has been assumed this is because biological factors predispose boys to be at greater risk for language-related disorders. As the basic foetus is female, with additions for males, it makes for greater complexity and more possibility of things going wrong in boys' development.

However, there is evidence that schools play a role in this outcome. In a USA study, teachers were asked to identify children with learning difficulties and a preponderance of boys resulted. When tests alone were used to identify such children, the male predominance was substantially reduced (Shaywitz and co-workers, 1990). Similar data was reported by Wadsworth and co-workers (1992) for samples of children with reading difficulties, both in the USA and UK. Cline and Reason (1993) noted that in the Shaywitz study, children identified with reading problems by teachers, but not by researchers, were more likely to have behaviour problems in school. This implies that teachers were misdiagnosing children as having reading problems because of their generally poor or disruptive behaviour – such problems were not picked up by researchers who had not experienced the bad behaviour. So it would seem that if children are a nuisance, it is more likely that 'learning problems' are identified and acted upon.

Special needs

Croll and Moses (1985) examined the incidence of special needs in mainstream schools and found the ratio of boys to girls was 2:1 overall, although with discipline problems the ratio rose to 4:1. Boys outnumber girls by a large margin in schools for children with emotional and behavioural difficulties, but by a smaller amount in those for profound learning difficulties and hearing problems (Riddell, 1996).

Comment

The evidence suggests that school is not such a rosy experience if you are male. Physical, mental, emotional and social reasons account for this. At a time when boys are preoccupied with their massive physical growth, there are increasing demands for them to concentrate on mental achievements. In the UK, an average child will complete 108 public tests by the time he leaves school and a bright one 125. Sports and other active pursuits have declined in state schools, having been squeezed out by an increasingly examination-biased agenda with pressure to perform academically. This is against nature, as the time from 10 to 17 years of age is the period when males, particularly, need plenty of activity in line with their rate of physical growth. They must be frustrated by the ever-increasing times for which they are required to sit still in class, so it is perhaps little wonder that they are apparently queuing up for exclusions and places in schools for children with emotional and behavioural difficulties, where they can breathe a sigh of relief! Perhaps we should take a tip from public schools, where academic classes are held in the mornings and in the afternoons students choose from a variety of sports, military cadet training or community service.

Traditionally, boy–girl differences have led to separate schooling at the adolescent stage, but the current fashion for mixed teaching means we need to think about building more choices into the curriculum. The male competitive and female co-operative preferences may conflict and set up communication barriers and these must be resolved if we want to avoid difficulties in classroom practice.

TIP: Make these issues a top topic in staff discussions and work towards a more active curriculum that is more compatible with male needs.

◆ Race

I worked in a school in London that was popularly known as '57 Varieties' as there were 57 different races on the register! While the great majority of ethnic minority children live in urban areas, there has been a good deal of dispersal from the initial areas of settlement. Local authorities in English counties had one in seven primary schools and one in five secondary schools with more than 5 per cent ethnic minority students in 1997 (DfEE/QCA 1999, Table E). Overall, there are in excess of 11 per cent of such students in both urban and rural settings in the UK.

This rich racial mix has brought many rewards. It also demands respect and reflection on how to blend the different views and attitudes of people from different cultural backgrounds. People from other races, who speak English as their second language, have more difficulty finding and keeping jobs and lack welfare support, which makes their lives difficult (Caesar and co-workers, 1994). This leads to social and economic disadvantage as well as social stigma. Bullying and name-calling are common and teachers are unaware of the scale of these and the impact they have on victims (Cohn, 1987).

TIP: Be proactive rather than reactive to bullying and name-calling. Use stories to highlight the issues. Give students opportunities to learn skills of relating to peers (see references to COGS, circle time and nurture groups on page 124). Set up a student council to deal with harassment, with a slot for playground events.

There is strong evidence of the operation of institutional racism in the delivery of services to children, defined as:

... the collective failure of an organization to provide an appropriate and professional service to people because of their colour, culture or ethnic origin. It can be seen or detected in processes, attitudes and behaviour which amount to discrimination through unwitting prejudice, ignorance, thoughtlessness, and racial stereotyping which disadvantage minority ethnic people.

Macpherson Committee of Enquiry (1999)

When SEN provision expanded after the Second World War, it became clear that higher than expected numbers of children from minority ethnic backgrounds were in special educational programmes. This was true in the UK (Tomlinson, 1984) and the USA (Tucker, 1980). In Inner London special schools in 1971, 34 per cent of those on roll were immigrants compared to 17 per cent in mainstream schools (Coard, 1971). Although over-representation of these students has reduced over the years, it still remains, especially in special provision for students with emotional and behavioural difficulties and in the numbers of exclusions (Bourne and co-workers, 1995). Gillborn and Gipps (1996) report that African-Caribbean students are between four and six times more likely to be excluded than white children. Cummins (1989) argues that their academic difficulties may be partially due to the reinforcement by schools of '… the ambivalence and insecurity that many minority students tend to feel with regard to their cultural identity'.

Students may become *disabled* in a similar manner to that experienced by their ethnic communities as they become disempowered by the dominant group.

Cummins (1986) points out that, internationally, the minority groups who perform poorly at school are those discriminated against in society by the dominant group. Two examples are frequently quoted:

◆ Finnish students have traditionally performed poorly in Swedish schools, where they are perceived by many as having low status, but have done comparatively well in Australia where their social standing is higher (Troike, 1978).

◆ In Japanese schools, children of the outcast Burakumin group do poorly on average, but in the USA where the caste difference is not noticed they have done as well as other Japanese immigrants (Ogbu, 1978).

Four characteristics are important in determining the performance of minority groups in this context (Cummins, 1986):

◆ **Cultural/linguistic incorporation** – the extent to which the language and culture of minority students are incorporated into the curriculum

◆ **Community participation** – the extent to which parents and community participate in school

◆ **Pedagogy** – whether teaching is organized on a traditional, transmission 'chalk-and-talk' model or an interactive one with student participation

◆ **Assessment** – the extent to which the purpose of assessment is to locate the problem *within* the student so legitimizing poor progress, or *without* the student (that is, in the learning environment), thereby seeking changes in the social and learning situation to promote student progress.

Cummins suggests that these characteristics are examined along a continuum from 'intercultural orientation' at one end to 'conforming to the majority culture' at the other. Community participation appears to be important, as shown by studies reporting low correlations between teacher and parent assessments of social skills of children from ethnic minority populations, compared with high correlations of assessments of white children (Keller, 1988). This suggests differences in expectations, highlighting the importance of involving parents in assessment and intervention planning.

Cummins' four-point framework analyses the educational interactions that students have, in order to understand where difficulties might lie. There is plenty of evidence that patterns of interaction in school can reverse those that prevail in society at large, by promoting student confidence in their personal identity and ability to succeed personally and academically. For example, Lenny Henry is a popular British comedian, born in the West Midlands to Jamaican parents, who has confounded all odds and climbed to the top of his professional tree, becoming widely respected for his skill and for his charity work with Comic Relief. There are many such examples in British society today, bringing a fresh, powerful perspective and influence to the community.

TIP: Use the Cummins framework to consider practice in your school. Which dimensions are strong and which need development? How can you effect appropriate changes?

In continuing the debate, it is important to highlight some of the dilemmas involved in attempting to take account of cultural and ethnic diversity in education. Keogh and co-workers (1997) argue that:

… on one level the issue is simple: everyone's heritage is due respect and the ideal is to find strength in diversity and to capitalize on, rather than stigmatize, difference.

They point out, however, the unrecognized paradox that in being sensitive to diversity educators run the risk of stereotyping individuals and perhaps treating them as if they share common traits with others of similar history. Ethnic group differences are often regarded as markers of cultural ones, which is an oversimplification of the situation. It is important to appreciate the social and cultural differences that exist among people with the same cultural roots.

Ethnic identity tends to persist through time. My paternal great grandparents moved to England from Scotland and although my parents and myself were born in England, I still feel that I am Scots (and I have the kilt to prove it!). On the other hand, culture changes as individuals and groups modify beliefs and practices over time according to environmental pressures. The lifestyles, expectations and values of new immigrants are often quite different to those of subsequent generations that are born in the adopted country. Changes in dress are a case in point; many second generation Indian girls in the UK wear Western-style trousers, for example, instead of the saris of their mothers. This is not to say, however, that their Indian identity has been lost. There are many other changes of lifestyle as newcomers seek to integrate with their new homeland. Remember the old adage 'When in Rome, do as Rome does'; this philosophy helps acceptance in a different milieu.

This evidence suggests the importance of distinguishing between ethnicity and culture in educational practice, and acknowledging variation at three levels:

- ◆ between ethnically defined groups
- ◆ within ethnically defined groups
- ◆ between individuals within ethnic and cultural groups.

Group disability

Issues of group disability and empowerment, as well as concerns about stereotyping, arise in intense form when there are racial differences between groups that parallel ethnic and/or cultural differences. Black groups in Europe and the USA were markedly over-represented in special needs contexts in schools (ILEA, 1983), propelling the Inner London Education Authority in the UK to introduce a framework for assessing racism which looked at practice and curriculum in schools and colleges. Three developmental dimensions on racism were outlined, the first being the earliest observed in British education and the last the one to which the authority aspired. Each dimension is regarded as an area of emphasis and not a separate, exclusive category because in most situations there will be overlap. The dimensions are:

◆ assimilation

◆ cultural diversity

◆ equality.

TIP: Rate your school on a scale of 1–3 for each of the three dimensions above (1= good, 2 = adequate, 3 = needs attention). How do staff attitudes and motivation towards racial issues, and their abilities to identify these dimensions, differ within your school?

Special needs and special educational needs

The Warnock Report (1978) on the special needs of children and young people had this to say about those with ethnic backgrounds:

Any tendency for educational difficulties to be assessed without proper reference to a child's cultural and ethnic background and its effect on his education can result in a category of handicap becoming correlated with a particular group in society.

As there is evidence that certain groups are over-represented in particular types of SEN provision, does this indicate that educational difficulties are generally *not* currently assessed with reference to a child's ethnic and cultural background and its effect on their education? There is widespread agreement internationally, and below are two examples from the UK.

In 1972, the proportion of all UK children in schools for moderate learning difficulties (MLD) was 0.6 per cent. The proportion of Caribbean children in MLD schools was 3.0 per cent (Tomlinson, 1982).

Although the gap has decreased, it remains large for children with emotional and behavioural disorders (Cooper and co-workers, 1994).

In 1985, the incidence of special needs among Asian and Caribbean students was 50 per cent greater than among white children. The incidence of discipline problems among Caribbean children was three times greater than for white students; the incidence among white students was twice that among Asians (Croll and Moses, 1985).

Given the disproportionate number of ethnic minority students in special education programmes, Artiles and co-workers (1997) argued for frameworks that explain interactions between socio-cultural variables and disability. Their proposals go beyond the current system of 'diagnosis, eligibility and placement' and recommend eliminating classifications for mild disabilities and notions of eligibility. 'Referrals' would thus become 'requests for assistance', to be met by learning support teams. Graf (1992) describes the role and goal of a learning support team:

 to assist *all* students without validating eligibility for special education

 to amalgamate mainstream and special education

 to co-ordinate activities of professionals in and out of school (educational psychologists no longer to *qualify* students for special provision but to act as school consultants).

The Green Paper, *Excellence for All Children* (DfEE, 1997), incorporates many of these ideas, focusing on policies aimed at raising standards for all students and on different professionals working together in mainstream education to provide necessary support.

Language issues

The language problems experienced by bilingual children living in the UK, who have English as an additional language (EAL), arise because they are living in a largely monolingual society. Competence in their first language does not help them communicate with most of the people they meet. There is, however, limited support for them to learn English. Barriers to learning arise from variations in word meanings, the use of tone and people's differing perceptions of the world.

It is interesting to note that English has around 60 words to describe feelings whereas Indian languages have in excess of 600. There is a striking difference in emphasis here, with the East far more developed than the West in expressing emotion. When teaching Chinese students, I was amazed to learn that vowel sounds in their language have about 12 tones, each one expressing a different meaning. The disparity between such a tonal language and the stress-timed dynamics of English must be confusing! One way of addressing these general issues is through a programme such as the Communication Opportunity Group Scheme (Sage, 2000), which has been mentioned in other contexts. Children with EAL must have opportunities to learn the rules of language and communication in a structured way that is relevant to their interests and concerns.

Even so, it is inevitable that just as some monolingual children have severe problems in speech, language and communication, so too will a number of bilingual children. These children almost certainly have difficulties in their first language as well as their second. The recognition of this may be delayed, because the people who work with the children are uncertain (Ofsted, 1997). These children tend to be referred to speech and language therapists when they are older than monolingual children with the same problems (Winter, 1999). A national survey of children in language units found that bilingual students had more severe problems than monolinguals and progressed less quickly (Crutchley and co-workers, 1997). There is now increasing interest in this issue; it is routinely covered in some texts (Martin, 2000) and guidance on assessment is offered with greater frequency (Madhani, 1994).

TIP: Be alert to any bilingual child who communicates less well than his peers and refer for speech and language assessment without delay. (I have found that bilingual children with communication difficulties also respond extremely well to the COGS approach, and this can be carried out in the context in which a child learns, either by a teacher, teaching assistant or learning mentor.)

A source of possible confusion is that some children develop their first language (L1) normally until they start to learn their second (L2). L1 is then arrested or even lost as they use L2 more in school. They are then diagnosed with specific language impairment if they are perceived to have difficulty in both languages. Schiff-Myers (1992) states that the error will be avoided if their early language history is recorded and includes:

◆ a description of the language(s) used at home

◆ age and conditions under which L2 was learned

◆ ages at which language milestones were reached in L1 before exposure to L2

◆ a description of family contacts with the country of origin

◆ motivation to be proficient in both languages.

TIP: A support teacher or a teaching assistant, experienced in interviewing parents, should investigate the language history as the first step towards understanding communication problems in a particular child.

Another source of uncertainty is that phonological and linguistic demands vary between languages. This means that something which would be no problem in learning one language may lead to problems in another. For example, a Chinese child who confuses tones will experience semantic (meaning) and syntactic (word arrangement) confusions that would not occur in English, because in Chinese languages syntax is partly signalled by tonal variations, while in English it is not. In Chinese, a tone can change a noun to a verb (for example, 'seed' to 'plant') or determine the direction of an event (for example, 'buy' to 'sell') (Zubrick, 1992).

Cline (1997) discusses a number of options to meet the language and cultural needs of children with EAL (see overleaf). Options 1–5 are described as *additive* – with L2 language teaching as a separate extra to normal provision. Option 6 is defined as *interactive* – with L1 and L2 both used in teaching and L1 and L2 developed within the curriculum. It is presently only available in the USA.

Option 1: additive	Curriculum teaching in L2 adapted for special needs
Option 2: additive	Curriculum teaching in L2 adapted *plus* in-class support/withdrawal
Option 3: additive	Curriculum teaching in L2 adapted *plus* in-class support/withdrawal *plus* part-time teaching in L1 of some curriculum aspects
Option 4: additive	Curriculum teaching in L2 adapted *plus* in-class support/withdrawal with adaptations for special needs
Option 5: additive	Curriculum teaching in L2 adapted *plus* in-class support/withdrawal with adaptations *plus* part-time teaching in L1 of some curriculum aspects with adaptations
Option 6: interactive	Teaching of L1 and L2 through curriculum teaching in L1 and L2 with adaptations

Options 3, 5 and 6 involve teaching in L1 as well as L2. At the moment, options 2 and 4 are more common but schools could aspire to 3 and 5, for children from their largest local community language groups, in the interest of school progress. Cline points out that additive options pose a risk that school experience will be fragmented. Also, opportunities for enhancing learning through consolidation and planned interplay of different elements will be lost.

Gadhok (1994) suggests the choice of options should take into account the parents' command of L1 and L2. There is obviously much to think about when planning for bilingual children, which requires more training for school staff and better links between EAL and SEN professionals.

With regard to language development, the education of deaf children from ethnic and linguistic minorities presents particular challenges. This group is growing quickly. A recent survey reported that almost 19 per cent of under-fives with sensori-neural hearing loss in England were from ethnic minority backgrounds; in 12 Inner London boroughs, these accounted for over half of this population (Turner, 1996). Over-representation was marked in the case of children from South Asian communities.

Diagnosis is generally delayed; Sharma and Love (1991) quoted an Indian parent who took her son to the GP for slow speaking:

His response was to say that our bilingual household was holding back [my son's] language development.

Limited numbers of staff who can converse in minority languages, and lack of interpreting services to help parents communicate with specialists, compound the problem (Turner, 1996). Surveys in the UK (Powers, 1996) and USA (Holt and Allen, 1989) have shown that deaf children from ethnic minority communities perform academically significantly less well than similar white children. Cohen and co-workers (1990) and Meherali, (1994) suggest measures to help cope with this problem, which include:

◆ reversing negative teacher attitudes and expectations

◆ improving parent–teacher communication

◆ celebrating ethnic minority traditions within the curriculum

◆ clarifying issues in a language policy

◆ supporting teachers to gain knowledge and commitment

◆ providing information in community languages.

These strategies have a school focus, but there are many factors outside school that depress performances. Many children experience 'socio-cultural dissonance', which is stress and a sense of incongruity caused by belonging to two cultures – a minority and the dominant one (Chau, 1989). Also, minority groups often have tight family relationships, perhaps to help protect them from the perceived threats of the world, which makes it difficult for their members to share their experiences with those outside this circle.

In concluding this section on language, it is pertinent to mention research on social skills, which are involved in the use of language for communication. Foster and co-workers (1996) discuss ethnically related differences in children's social behaviour along four dimensions:

❶ Orientation towards the group – interdependent and co-operative versus individual and competitive

❷ Attitudes towards authority – deferential versus equalitarian

❸ Communication style – expressive versus constrained

❹ Coping style – active versus passive.

Different ethnic groups in the USA have been located on these dimensions. Blacks are more interdependent and co-operative, deferential and expressive than whites. Both groups are more active compared with Asian or Spanish children. There is a great deal of variation in scores, so educators need to be sensitive to different cultural expectations and resist stereotypes in their perceptions of students.

TIP: Spend a minute considering the four dimensions above in relation to two or more different race children in your class. How do they differ? How would you use this information in planning group activity?

Working with parents

Working with parents has been woven into the discussion in the previous section, but deserves a separate mention. There is a need to be sensitive to ethnic group differences in parents' beliefs about education and goals for their children. What works in some families may not work in others. Huss-Keeler (1997) reported a study in a northern England urban school where 80 per cent of students were from Punjabi-speaking Pakistani families. Parents from this community were interested in their children's learning but demonstrated this very differently from middle-class white parents. Teachers misinterpreted their responses as a lack of interest.

Frederickson and Cline (2002) report a study in a similar community in southern England. Parents' experience of maths learning differed greatly from their children's, in the ways they were taught to do arithmetic. Success in supporting their children's learning depended on how they negotiated the gap between old and new strategies. This applied to both monolingual and bilingual parents but for the latter group, uncertainties about the use of language for maths was a major concern.

Both studies noted that teachers appeared to be unaware of the importance of parents' worries. Concerns such as those described are reinforced when ethnic and linguistic minority parents read news reports about failing schools and their ethnic compositions, which seem to imply that the presence of minorities lowers standards. This has the effect of distancing parents from institutions – they need a very welcoming approach from schools to encourage them to become more involved.

TIP: Make opportunities to talk to parents on a regular basis, so that they can keep in touch with what is going on in school. Encourage them to clarify issues that concern them. Do not assume they will approach you spontaneously to air their worries.

Points about teaching

In the last section, issues surrounding the teaching of maths are mentioned, and it is useful to expand on these at this juncture.

Maths is described as abstract, international or universal. In teaching, there is an assumption of a uniform mathematical representation of human experience across all cultural groups. Researchers have identified diverse skills and approaches to calculation among children in different countries. They have demonstrated that the same children adopt different strategies for mathematical tasks, depending on whether they are working in school or in a family or street enterprise. Abreu (1995) suggested the social value given to different forms of practice was a crucial factor.

In our multicultural society, it is helpful if the school curriculum makes reference to the diverse mathematical traditions that are represented in the various ethnic group cultures of its students. As a student teacher, I was fascinated how this was presented in a Leicester school, where I was on practice. There was an Egyptian boy in the class, who was the focus of a project on maths from his part of the world. Many mathematical secrets were revealed in pyramid tomes. We ended up making a mummy and calculating the length of cloth required to wind it up for burial, using counting sticks. It was active and fun, providing a new perspective on the use of mathematics in another part of the world. Other ideas are Vedic arithmetic, which enhances the understanding of number; Islamic Art patterns, presenting complex geometric construction; and the Chinese rod numeral method of solving simultaneous equations, leading naturally to methods used in higher maths.

An example of how the idea of using maths traditions from different cultures has been put into practice is the SMILE scheme (Secondary Mathematics Individualized Learning Experience), which I used as a teacher. It is a set of individualized materials, developed in London, and widely used in schools (ILEA, 1990). The development team of practising teachers published an anti-racist policy for the scheme, which has generally been followed (Monaghan, 1999) and can be used for all subject teaching. This advocates:

◆ strong emphasis on the historical development of maths, showing how this results from problems that needed to be solved (Indian astronomers, Egyptian farmers, Spanish navigators, and so on)

◆ that maths of the developing world be made accessible to all children

◆ that maths content be made relevant to a multicultural society.

The SMILE materials reflect a range of contributions to maths from all parts of the world, as well as presenting Britain positively as a multiracial society. The only downside is that these individualized activities require independent skills and good language levels. There is as much reading as maths required, which defeats some students. I supported the SMILE work in class, and my students were not always smiley! Nevertheless, the scheme is a brilliant conception and worth exploring for its rationale.

To conclude this section, it is worth quoting a set of inclusive, collaborative learning strategies that are useful in pursuing multicultural approaches in the classroom, suggested by Joseph (1993).

◆ Draw on students' own experience as a resource in lessons.

◆ Recognize different cultural heritages in the lesson content.

◆ Combat racism by producing positive images of others.

◆ Promote socially desirable attitudes.

When children from ethnic or linguistic minority communities experience learning difficulties in school, one contributing factor is the way the curriculum is taught in an exclusive rather than inclusive way, with narrow perspectives that do not reflect diversity. The approach discussed here may be contrasted with that of the working party responsible for the maths national curriculum framework in England, which was sceptical of the value of inclusive ideas (DES, 1988).

Comment

A key question, therefore, is whether any analysis or intervention can measure up to the diversity of minorities and the challenges of racism that they face. Over time, groups will become broader and less heterogeneous, and more likely to respond to an interactional approach that is sensitive to the cultural context. There are many things we can do to help reduce the problems that children from different races experience in our schools. That so many members of our immigrant populations are successful in all walks of life is a tribute to their determination and the education they have received. Nevertheless, there are many barriers they have to surmount and it is a concern that there are disproportionate numbers of ethnic minority students in special education provision. Changes are possible and can be accelerated by positive attitudes in schools, which have the power to do a great deal to reverse unhelpful practices.

◆ Review

There are complex and often puzzling differences and difficulties in class, gender and racial groups. It is essential that both *within-* and *without-the-child* factors are carefully analysed as a base for deciding action. Social class issues are divisive in education and children from lower classes are severely emotionally, socially and academically disadvantaged when compared with middle and upper levels. In England, the national curriculum, with its age-related tests, ranks and orders children as never before and their value to school and workplace will vary accordingly. This reinforces class distinctions strongly in ways that prevent social mobility.

Girls appear to be outperforming boys, who may be disadvantaged by the increasing emphasis on an academic curriculum. For most of their schooling, boys' physical development is their natural focus and they need a more active programme than is presently on offer. The male competitive and female co-operative preferences conflict and set up communication barriers, which can be pronounced in school settings and is the reason why the sexes have been traditionally separated for their adolescent years. With mixed teaching, there must be more choices as the 'one size fits all' philosophy clearly cannot cope with diverse needs.

Britain has a rising immigrant population and absorbing different races is challenging for us all. Around us, there is evidence of people from different ethnic backgrounds being highly successful and there are many in powerful positions who can offer a new perspective to British life. There is a disproportionate number of immigrants, however, in special education provision and we need to address the policies and practices that are preventing these students from fulfilling their potential. Language development is an important need for the bulk of bilingual students as there are few facilities to give them opportunities to learn to communicate well in English, and their general lack of skills is undoubtedly depressing academic performances. Being aware of the real situation brings the impetus for change, which requires an integrated approach, involving students, families, schools and communities in solving the wide range of problems diversity brings.

Main Points

- ◆ Class plays an important role in deciding status, and the lower levels are seriously socially and economically disadvantaged with clear implication for school success.

- ◆ Class divisions are strengthened by the national curriculum in England, which ranks children as never before and stifles opportunities for the lower socio-economic groups.

- ◆ Girls outperform boys at school; it appears that the curriculum is more suited to their needs, as it involves a high verbal content and co-operative styles of learning.

- ◆ Boys need more physical outlets during their schooling to meet their requirements for competitive activity.

- ◆ The fact that British society is becoming increasingly multiracial suggests a need for a curriculum that *includes* rather than *excludes* students; at present, children's cultural heritage is not given much attention in the content of lessons.

- ◆ Diversity has many dimensions; only an integrative approach between schools, families and the community will provide the resources to meet the huge variety of student needs.

Chapter Four

What are disabilities and learning difficulties?

Overview

In England, the number of children identified as having learning difficulties has increased over 40 per cent since the national curriculum came on stream and certain academic standards became expected from all our children. This situation brings into focus the problems that children have with learning due to physical, mental, emotional and social causes. This chapter unpicks the issues, particularly with regard to the assessment and management of children, while Appendix 4 (page 131) provides a description of the main learning difficulties and medical conditions that affect children's progress in school.

◆ Introduction

There are so many labels used to describe children these days that it's easy to become confused as to what they all really mean. Diagnostic and descriptive terms also seem to change frequently – just as you get used to an expression, it is dropped in favour of a new one. And so it goes on. 'Disability' is just such a label, now enshrined in the Disability Discrimination Act (DTI, 1995), which aims to end inequity against this minority group in society. Other terms with similar meanings include 'defect', 'deficit', 'disorder', 'handicap', 'abnormality' and 'impairment'. They all refer to the same condition: an inability to function in what is considered a normal way because of biological disturbances.

The term 'disability', however, brings confusion. Take the case of Bobby. He is a ten-year-old spastic quadriplegic – he has a type of cerebral palsy causing stiffness and rigidity in body movements. In Bobby's case, the condition affects all four limbs. It is a non-progressive, but permanent, movement disability so Bobby needs a wheelchair to get around and a communication aid to speak. He is a very bright boy, achieving level 5 on his Key Stage 2 tests in primary school (national curriculum in England), and is above the norm for his age. His Mum (a single parent) was thinking about his secondary schooling; the authorities wanted him to attend a provision for the physically disabled, 12 miles away. There are no other students as bright as Bobby in this school, and few achieve GCSEs. The local comprehensive would meet his academic needs better but is on two levels with no lifts, so the professionals involved in the case felt it was not suitable.

Bobby's Mum took the authority to tribunal. Her argument was that although Bobby has a permanent neurological condition affecting mobility, this does not disable him because he uses a wheelchair and has a communication aid, which allows him to be independent. Her view was that the *school* would be disabling him by not offering the facilities for moving from one level to another. The dilemmas are obvious. Here, the focus on context demands led to an analysis of disabling environments with hostile attitudes, rather than thinking of Bobby, his functioning and excellent abilities. As a wheelchair user, he has no mobility problems. His mobility, however, would be hampered by an inappropriate building design. He was being discriminated against in terms of access. The new disability law was on his side and Bobby won the tribunal case. The comprehensive school must make it possible for him to access lessons.

The use of the term 'disability' causes problems because of the way we perceive the difficulties to be within the child rather than to do with the situation. Research suggests that teachers do not believe environmentally focused explanations of learning problems. Croll and Moses (1985) found that primary teachers, who were asked to give explanations for classroom learning and behaviour difficulties, cited within-child factors and rarely considered school to be responsible. This is a clear example of a well-established tendency to over-attribute the behaviour of other people to their personal characteristics and underestimate the effects of the situation.

TIP: Have you got a disabled child in your class? In what ways does the context discriminate against her? Are there ways to improve the situation?

◆ Analysing child development and difficulties

A child's development and difficulties can be described in a simple interactive framework that offers three levels of description and the operation of environmental and school management factors. This framework is modelled opposite in defining Bobby's situation. Therapists and psychologists working with children with developmental problems employ such levels of analysis and Frith (1995) describes their use with dyslexic students.

Interactive description of Bobby's development and difficulties		
Environment		Management
	Biological	
	Spastic quadriplegia due to neurological damage sustained during birth trauma	Taxi to school, wheelchair
Decongestant medication	Intermittent conductive hearing loss	Talk to face
	Cognitive	
May need technical support	Above average thinking shown using output from aids	Word processor with joy stick
Adapt oral tasks for speech synthesizer	Uses narrative communication	Speech synthesizer
	Expresses feelings appropriately	
	Behavioural	
Minimal assistance with eating and toilet	Gross and fine motor skills disturbed	Alternatives to field sports (canoeing), practical tasks need adapting
	English level 5 (reads at 14-year-old level), maths level 5, science level 5	

◆ **Biological level**: This records brain or body abnormalities, and sensory processes such as hearing and vision.

◆ **Cognitive level**: Cognitive skills or deficits can only be inferred from behaviour, and include thinking activities such as perception, memory, problem solving with its expression in feelings and ideas, words, and so on.

◆ **Behavioural level**: This records facts about practical and academic performance. Environmental factors such as classroom work, ethos and student motivation affect behaviour.

◆ **Environment**: This identifies general needs for support, such as medicine for congestion and speech synthesizer.

◆ **Management**: Curriculum issues are specified for each level and, although there is some overlap with 'Environment' support, this section focuses on work rather than general issues.

TIP: Is this framework relevant for you? If so, try it to analyse the development and difficulties of an appropriate student.

◆ Defining learning difficulties

The revised Code of Practice (DfES, 2001) has removed any categorical division between moderate (IQ range 51–70) and severe (IQ range 0–50) levels of learning difficulty. These descriptions were based on IQ divisions but were discredited when special schools showed a student population significantly wider than the range (Yule, 1975). A framework based on Sternberg's (1985) analysis of ability (see pages 35–36) draws on teachers' knowledge of expected levels of performance with the national curriculum for England as a key reference point. Guidance is now available regarding a more detailed analysis of progress towards Level 1 (QCA, 2001).

Much of the language used in defining learning difficulties historically has been based on the premise that the difficulty is *within the child*. Booth and Ainscow (1998), along with others, have argued that a *social* view of difficulties is preferable. Learning difficulties arise in a relationship between students and tasks and the resources available to support learning. This empowers teachers to make the adaptations needed to their own practices and classrooms.

Resolute ideas about ability and educability suggest that limited attainment reflects a ceiling determined by factors beyond teachers' control. It gives the impression that a group of children exists whose potential and needs are different from the majority. This makes teachers doubt their own expertise and resources. Tomlinson (1988) highlighted the lack of agreement among professionals about what constitutes educational subnormality, analysing their responses in the framework below.

Why Johnny can't read (Tomlinson,1988)	
Level 1: Personal/Interpersonal	Because he's thick; He can't concentrate; He doesn't like his teacher
Level 2: Environmental/Institutional	He's got a disadvantaged background; He lives in an inner-city area; The school hasn't got the right staff/resources/methods to teach reading
Level 3: Structural/Societal	He's black and working class; Schools help to reproduce cultural, social and economic inequalities

Tomlinson says that teachers and psychologists have tended to use level 1 and 2 explanations, while theorists have attempted to move the focus to level 3, placing problems in wider contexts. These views about learning problems have been reflected in assessment rationales.

◆ Assessment

Four approaches to assessment are discussed below, which vary according to the ways problems are conceptualized. These approaches focus on:

◆ the learner
◆ the zone of proximal development
◆ the learning environment
◆ the teaching programme.

Focus on the learner – traditional assessment approach

The conventional approach to assessing learning difficulties has been to use normative assessments, in which results are compared with a representative sample to produce a standard score. The aim is to determine the category of difficulty, based on the assumption that the source of the problems is within the child, with test performance compared to age norms. The pattern of strengths and weaknesses that emerge are intended to form the basis of a teaching programme that uses strengths to build on weaknesses.

The belief that such assessments provides scientific evidence is refuted on the basis of the arbitrary nature of the tasks and the artificiality of the testing procedures, which seldom reflect normal activities. The act of comparing children's performance to an age-related norm cannot help teachers to identify what they have already learned and what they need to learn next. So the information is of limited value in planning an educational programme. Such tests tell us little about the processes that underpin competence. They ignore functions that have not yet matured but are in the process of doing so. Assessment is essentially retrospective rather than prospective. This suggests that a dynamic approach is needed.

Focus on the zone of proximal development – dynamic assessment approach

This approach defines the difference between what children can achieve alone and the level they can reach with adult help. The view is that emerging skills provide a better estimate of an individual's potential for succeeding beyond the present level. The focus is on the child's performance and the amount and kind of help required to achieve it.

Dynamic approaches to assessment are based on a social constructionist view of development, derived from Vygotsky's idea that higher order mental processes develop from co-operating with others, only later becoming inner, individual functions of the child (Vygotsky, 1978). The role of a more knowledgeable other person is crucial in providing assistance, finely tuned to what is already known and can be achieved. Learning is thus constructed through joint interaction with the emphasis on *potential* rather than maturity or readiness.

Static tests, such as those that measure intelligence, evaluate what has already been learned – the 'zone of actual development' (ZAD). It is more useful to assess the 'zone of proximal development' (ZPD) using dynamic measures to do so. For example, suppose the performance of two students on a static test is the same, both scoring at a ten-year-old level. They are then

71

re-tested using standard questions with prompts towards the correct solutions to problems they could not solve before. One child scores at an 11-year-old level, while the second achieves that of a 12 year old. This is seen as the difference between the ZAD (what can be achieved alone) and the ZPD (what is achieved with help). In this instance, one child has greater emerging skills and knowledge than the other and demonstrates more scope for enhancing his attainments (Vygotsky, 1978).

In the West, claims have been made for dynamic approaches to assessment in relation to children from ethnic and linguistic minorities. Static tests are seen to penalize children who have had limited opportunities to learn what is being tested (Feuerstein, 1979). By building coaching into the process of testing, dynamic assessment counterbalances inequalities in experience and is less prone to bias.

Different users of the dynamic assessment approach have various aims. Budoff (1987) used it to classify children more accurately for special educational placement. On the basis of standard procedure, he analysed children as:

◆ **high performers**: who perform well without support and only marginally improve with coaching

◆ **gainers**: who initially perform poorly but make gains after coaching

◆ **non-gainers**: who initially perform poorly and gain little from coaching.

There was interest in identifying children who had been classified as being of limited ability but who proved to be *gainers* in these assessments.

Probably the best use of dynamic assessment methods, however, is to plan instruction as effectively as possible.

The assessment process can be arranged in various ways – for example, it may involve daily sessions over a week, or 'pre-test', 'coaching' and 'post-test' phases on one occasion. The core of the method is the coaching phase, which itself can take a number of forms, such as:

◆ simple feedback on correct performance

◆ demonstration of the correct solution to the problem with or without explanation

◆ prompts or hints in the form of questions.

The coaching could be standardized and the same for all, or tailored to the needs of each child individually. Feuerstein (1979) practised a high degree of individualization in the coaching phase. Critics highlight the risk of this strategy, as decision making is subjective for both test administration and interpretation. It takes time to train in the method, as well as time to use it with a child. Inter-tester reliability is untested and suspect (Missiuna and Samuels, 1988). A solution is to use computer technology, in a procedure where the kinds of errors made by the subject determine the prompts and items presented next. The key point is that, while each child has a different experience, there are standard rules embedded in the program (Guthke and co-workers, 1997).

What is measured?

With conventional intelligence tests the final score is usually a quotient formed by comparing the sum of items passed with age norms. With dynamic assessment there are various measurement possibilities: post-test score after coaching; difference score (between pre- and post-test); or measures based on coaching (number of items where help given, or number of hints given at request). There are reliability problems with all these measures.

In seeking to develop the dynamic assessment method, it is probably necessary to stop thinking of assessment and teaching processes as being separate, as is conventionally the case. Good practice requires an assessment–teaching–assessment cycle.

An alternative combines the advantages of assisted (dynamic) assessment with the psychometric standards of traditional tests. Sage (2000b) has produced an assessment in the dynamic model. In the Sage Assessment of Language and Thinking (SALT) there is a ten-question interview test for both children and adults, which can be scored conventionally or as an assisted process. The test takes 5–10 minutes, but even this is a long time for a busy educator. In reality, what is needed is a continuum of assessment possibilities with simple, quick screening at one end and more intensive, dynamic approaches at the other. The Communication Opportunity Group Scheme (COGS) (Sage, 2000a) includes a range of assessment methods in the manual, which can be chosen to suit the purpose required. A diagnostic, group-teaching assessment is also available (Sage, 2003).

Focus on the learning environment

This shifts emphasis onto the learning environment provided by school. Such assessment depends on observations, diary records, and questionnaires or interviews with students and teachers, in order to determine factors that may cause or exacerbate learning difficulties.

Focus on the teaching programme

The drive towards inclusive education has directed interest to the teaching in classrooms. The assumption is that the curriculum presented is not suited to the current learning needs of the child experiencing difficulties. The assessment approach requires that learning tasks are analysed and arranged into a hierarchy of component skill elements, to be tackled in incremental steps.

Bloom's (1956) taxonomy of educational objectives is useful and relevant here:

1. **knowledge** — facts, figures, information, observed and recalled situations
2. **comprehension** — perceiving, understanding, interpreting, comparing, contrasting, ordering
3. **application** — using knowledge, information, concepts, problem-solving strategies, techniques
4. **analysis** — perceiving patterns, relationships, components, hidden meanings

5 synthesis   relating, combining, inferring, predicting, generalizing, concluding

6 evaluation   comparing, contrasting, discriminating, assessing, prioritizing, verifying.

Students who learn slowly benefit from activities that target levels 1 and 2 and concentrate on *understanding* as well as *knowing* key facts. Others can extend their learning through application of knowledge from levels 4–6.

Able children should concentrate on levels 5 and 6, where they are encouraged to evaluate knowledge, make conclusions from evidence and give opinions on this. The ability to synthesize and appraise marks out the true scholar – one who can bring together information and stamp her own views on it. Very few students achieve this level at any stage of their education and this reflects a lack of opportunity to discuss issues and form opinions in oral exchanges where they can consider the ideas of others. Thus, the higher levels of thought are only possible through planned *talk* sessions that provide 'information gap' (exchanges to find solutions) and 'opinion gap' activities (feelings and experiences shared and defended) (Sage, 2000a: 45). This level of mental operation is essential for comprehension of complex talk and text.

Comment

The question is whether it is practical to put dynamic assessment and teaching into busy classrooms with the tremendous pressure and demands made on teachers today. Even if new information is gained there is no guarantee that it will be used. Elliott (2000) observes that in addition to the challenges of making time in a class schedule, there is uncertainty over how much systematic knowledge teachers require of the underlying theory and concepts in order to make sense of the tasks they face. However, Watson (2000) is optimistic, regarding this type of teaching assessment as promoting learning experiences in which:

- ◆ the learner is active, confident and aware of their learning
- ◆ the teacher is responsive to student interests and understanding
- ◆ learning is constructed through interaction, and talk about the task is emphasized
- ◆ teachers extend students' thinking through challenging tasks with high expectations
- ◆ through scaffolding and mediating, thinking is restructured and facilitated
- ◆ learners are helped to be self-directed and in control of their learning.

If some of these ideas are filtered through to practice in the hectic school day, life will be enhanced!

Mismatch between student need and help received

> The purpose of education for all children is the same; the goals are the same but the help children need in progressing towards them will be different.

Department of Education and Science (1978)

If there is a mismatch between the help students need and the help they receive, there will often be a culture of blame. The polarized assumptions are summarized in the table below.

Students failing school	Schools failing students
Limited communication skills	Inadequate identification of need
Limited literacy and numeracy	Inappropriate teaching
Poor behaviour, motivation and attendance	Inappropriate curriculum
Lack of confidence and self-image	Uninspiring environment
Low parent expectations	Low teacher expectations
Lack of parent support	Unfavourable student-to-staff ratio
Social deprivation	Lax discipline

Christenson and Ysseldyke (1989) emphasized that the learning environment for a child in class is influenced by key features in the wider context, but they appeared to ignore aspects such as neighbourhood subcultures and ethnic and linguistic communities. A possible model placing learning in context is presented here.

School	Classroom	Home	Community
Inclusive philosophy	Choices to meet diverse needs	Participation	Involvement
Staff collaboration	Organization and management	Support for learning	Opportunities to extend learning
Personal and academic focus	Balanced curriculum	All learning valued	Workplace–school liaison
Curriculum decisions	Curriculum implementation	Curriculum support	Extra expertise and support
Teaching resources	Resources matched to needs	Home supplements	Libraries, museums and so on
Support services	Specific programmes	Specific support	Expertise: charities and so on

Successful support for children with learning difficulties is very dependent on the quality of special expertise available both inside and outside school, and the ability of parents to reinforce learning at home. Unfortunately, there are limited numbers of specifically trained teachers, and therapists are always overburdened by medical as well as educational cases. Sage and Sommefeldt (2004) found, in a pilot study of 300 school staff, that less than 1 per cent had accredited training in special educational needs according to national standards and most teachers relied on picking up knowledge from whatever source was available. Sage and Cwenar (2003) found that 50 per cent of teachers and 75 per cent of support staff felt they did not have the skills to help all children learn. Appendix 4 (page 131) provides information about the common learning and medical problems found in classes in the UK and gives tips on general handling and class management as a baseline resource for educators.

◆ The gap between theory and practice

Research and theory, outlined in this book, have important practical implications for assessment and intervention for students with SEN. Scant attention is paid to environmental issues in learning, so that many students fail to achieve their potential because the context is not suitable for their particular needs. Sources frequently comment on the gap between theory and practice, and McKee and Witt (1990) consider two aspects of the issue:

◆ **social and political problems** – the difficulty of targeting instructional issues that are considered the domain of teachers rather than researchers

◆ **technical problems** – the difficulty of communicating information to teachers in a way that is helpful and enabling.

The national curriculum in England, with its concomitant regular school inspections, has changed the construction of the class as being exclusively the educators' domain. Now educators are accountable to the child, parents and the community, and are expected to embrace continuing professional development in order to meet changing demands. Increasing amounts of evidence about effective learning are readily available, but staff feel they do not have time to access information (Sage and Cwenar, 2003). This factor represents the greatest barrier of all to successful assessment and intervention of children with special educational needs; school leaders and governing bodies *must* give teaching and support staff encouragement and opportunity to continue their own learning.

◆ Review

Disability has produced a large vocabulary of descriptive terms that have changed over time in line with political correctness. The problem with labels is that they restrict views and prevent broad approaches to assessment and management. Identification of special educational needs requires a framework that considers not only biological, cognitive and behavioural factors but also environmental and management issues. Traditionally, tests have located within-the-child factors that have dominated intervention, but more dynamic assessment is likely to provide a broader, more accurate picture of a child's potential by incorporating environmental perspectives that lead to more effective instruction.

Teaching of children with SEN requires that learning tasks are analysed and arranged into a hierarchy of component skill elements, to ensure that students are given activities that are relevant for their abilities. Evidence suggests that students at all levels of the education system are limited in their ability to synthesize and evaluate information, which is indicative of a lack of opportunities to discuss opinions orally, hear a range of views and make judgements about these.

There is a gap between research knowledge and practice, and schools are not using information that could make their work more effective for all concerned. School leaders and governing bodies need to encourage and provide more opportunities for staff professional development that has both a theoretical and practical orientation.

Main Points

- Labels to describe disability can restrict assessment and intervention approaches, and limit a child's potential.
- Assessment must consider biological, cognitive and behavioural factors within the context of environmental and management issues.
- Traditional assessment does not help teachers plan learning, and more dynamic approaches must be encouraged to focus on child potential.
- Learning tasks must be analysed and arranged into a hierarchy of skills, and teachers ensure that students are given activities appropriate to their level of development.
- The gap between research knowledge and practice needs bridging so that students and professionals can benefit from evidence available on what strategies work best.

General Attainment Profile – from The Communication Opportunity Group Scheme (Sage, 2000a)

		Stage 1	Stage 2	Stage 3
Personal qualities	Consideration	Sometimes considers/helps others	Maintains courtesy/consideration with support	Behaves courteously and considerately always
	Motivation	Shows some interest/persistence	Maintains interest/persistence with support	Responds with motivation and persistence
Social qualities	Accepting responsibility	Needs support to accept responsibility	Accepts responsibility when duties are defined and straightforward	Accepts responsibility using sound judgement and initiative
	Working independently	Needs step-by-step guidance and continual support	Works independently with general guidance	Works independently from instruction
	Working in a group	Needs support/guidance to work in a group	Responds but does not initiate in group actions	Works constructively, initiating ideas and actions
Decision making	Attaining information	Needs guidance to find information	Uses standard sources independently	Seeks and gathers information from a variety of sources
	Planning	Needs prompting to prepare sequenced activities	Chooses from alternatives the best way to tackle tasks	Shows originality in creating new plans
	Problem solving	Accepts situations without criticism	Assesses basic problems and seeks solutions independently	Evaluates and solves complex problems
	Evaluating results	Relies on other to assess results	Assesses results with assistance	Assesses results and identifies improvements
Communication	Listening	Shows some ability to listen to instructions	Listens and retains information	Listens, retains and analyses information
	Talking	Makes appropriate replies to questions	Initiates topics in conversation – uses questions and maintenance comments	Speaks fluently with a range of people and in different contexts describing, explaining and negotiating
	Reading	Reads/understands short, simple text	Reads/understands a variety of written forms	Selects/judges written evidence
	Writing	Writes short sentences clearly	Writes logically and descriptively	Discusses and evaluates concisely
Performance	Following instructions	Follows simple verbal/written instructions	Follows multi-step verbal/written forms	Follows complex information confidently
	Using equipment	Uses equipment to perform simple tasks with guidance	Selects and uses suitable equipment independently	Uses equipment, identifying and rectifying faults
	Accuracy/neatness	Sometimes produces neat, accurate work	Produces mainly neat, accurate work	Produces meticulous work
	Safety	Remembers safety instructions	Recognizes risks	Acts to reduce risks
Numeracy/ Information technology	Using numerals	Uses basic counting and number concepts	Uses basic techniques (+, –, ×, ÷) to solve problems	Calculates ratios, percentages and proportions
	Using signs/diagrams	Recognizes everyday signs and symbols	Uses maps, simple diagrams and timetables	Uses and interprets graphs, charts and technical drawings
	Using a computer	Understands a standard keyboard and uses a simple program with support	Uses a standard word processing package to create, retain and retrieve information for everyday purposes	Uses a disk to create, retain and retrieve information for a variety of purposes – e.g. word processing, spreadsheets. Uses internet facilities

Chapter Five

What key skills support learning?

Overview

In our drive to build children's knowledge for standard tests, we can easily forget the importance of rock solid foundations. These take time to lay down, but learning will soon disappear unless the key skills of processing, memorizing and responding to information are secure. This chapter considers how the key skills of communication and co-operation emerge from the interaction of physical, mental, emotional and social development. An assessment profile is provided (opposite).

◆ Introduction

What are the key skills that underpin learning? They are generally taken to include personal and social qualities, decision making, communication, performance and the use of numeracy and technology (Sage, 2000b). On page 78, opposite, is a profile to assess levels of competence in these. Our content-driven curriculum marginalizes some of these areas, but personal abilities underpin all learning so their development must be of prime concern to educators. This section outlines the main features of physical, mental, emotional and social development, which interrelate for the achievement of personal competences. Tasks and tips are provided to help readers facilitate learning for their own students.

◆ Physical development

Physical development sets limits not only on what children can experience, but also on what they can learn and how they can use this knowledge and understanding. Also, physical growth and change affects self-image and confidence in building relationships. The experiences and interactions of unusually small children, who develop slowly, may be different from those of bigger, faster-growing peers, especially in adolescence. At 14, I felt like an elephant alongside fairies because I had grown faster than my friends! A child compares his own self-image with an ideal in the head. Actual physical characteristics may be less important than the feelings we have about them. What are the aspects of growth that have impact on our learning?

Height and weight

A newborn baby is one-third of her final height, but the head is huge in relation to the body. By three, children are half their adult height. In adolescence, a growth spurt comes earlier for girls and is shorter than for boys, resulting in a lower average height for women. The growth of body parts progresses at different rates – hands and feet grow fastest, followed by arms and legs, with the trunk being the slowest, giving a gangly appearance and feelings of awkwardness during adolescence.

Bones and muscles

At birth, bones are soft, hardening at different rates. The hand and wrist stiffen first to grasp and pick up objects. Muscles change enormously in length and thickness. During adolescence there is a sharp increase in the amount of muscle tissue, particularly in boys, accompanied by a decrease in fat. Between 13 and 17 years of age, a boy's strength doubles and male–female differences become marked. This may be an issue in relation to academic performance. At a time when boys, especially, are preoccupied with physical growth and need constant exercise, they are being increasingly asked to concentrate on mental activities. This causes tension, as school demands do not follow nature.

Movement

A baby's ability to control muscles and move around is striking. The table below shows approximate milestones in motor development from a survey of child development norms operating in the UK (Sage, 1990). Co-ordination progresses from large to small body muscles and movements. The timing of development varies from one person to another and the table offers only a rough guide. Moving is directly linked to bone and muscle development. Until neck and trunk muscles have matured it is impossible to hold up the head or sit securely.

Approximate age when skill appears	Motor skill
1 month	Lifts chin while lying on stomach
2 months	Lifts chest as well as chin
4–6 months	Rolls over from lying position
7 months	Picks up objects using the palm without thumb and forefinger
8–9 months	Sits up easily
	Stands by holding onto something and then independently
12–15 months	Takes first steps
13–15 months	Grasps objects with thumb and forefinger
18 months	Walks well alone
2 years	Walks up and down stairs with both feet on each step
	Runs well
30 months	Walks on tiptoe
3 years	Rides a tricycle
4 years	Walks up and down stairs, one foot at a time
	Throws a ball overhand
4–5 years	Hops on one foot

Practice is vital to facilitate progress and, if children have limited opportunities, motor development will be slower (Brazelton and co-workers, 1969). Studies by Gesell and Thompson (1929) indicate that practice is only useful once a child is ready to perform a skill. Williams and Scott (1953) found poor, black infants in Washington D.C. demonstrating faster growth than those from middle-class families because they were less restricted and their parents more permissive. The maturational process sets limits on the rate of physical growth and motor development but this may be delayed by the absence of appropriate experience and practice. Hormones also have an effect on growth and have been discussed under the section on male–female differences (page 51).

TASK: Using the above guide, consider the motor development of two children you know.

◆ What are the similarities and differences in their maturation?

◆ What is the impact of their degrees of maturation on other development?

◆ Brain development

Brain growth has been less frequently and deeply considered than body development because it is not so easily seen. The three main brain areas are the cerebellum, the limbic brain and the cerebrum and cortex, as shown in the diagram below.

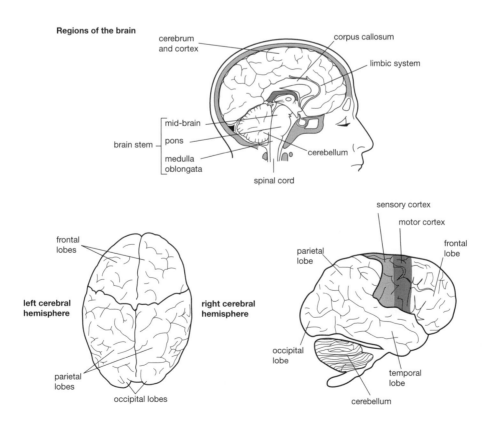

Approximate ages and stages of brain growth	
Conception to 15 months: cerebellum development	◆ survival systems: breathing, sleeping, waking, eating, elimination ◆ sensory development: balance, hearing, touch, smell and seeing ◆ motor development: reflexes integrate into movements of neck, arms and legs
15 months to 4.5 years: limbic system development	◆ emotional exploration: feelings, emotions and their expression ◆ social development: memory and relationships – self and others ◆ large movement proficiency: walking, running, jumping, climbing
4.5–7 years: global hemisphere development (usually right-brain)	◆ sees whole picture: top-down processing; makes deductions ◆ builds images from movement and feeling: rhythm, emotion, intuition ◆ talks to develop thoughts: outer speech
7–9 years: linear hemisphere development (usually left-brain)	◆ processes detail: bottom-up processing; induces from details ◆ develops complex language (clauses): understands sounds, letters, words in writing ◆ uses logic/linear processing to solve problems; develops techniques
8–9 years: frontal lobe development	◆ fine motor proficiency: manual dexterity for writing and two-dimensional eye focus (fovea) ◆ internal language formed to regulate tasks and behaviour (inner language)
9–12 years: increased connections between right- and left-brain (corpus callosum)	◆ right- and left-brain integration ◆ proficient top-down and bottom-up processing
12–16 years: hormonal changes of puberty	◆ body conscious: preoccupied with body functions of self and others ◆ increases social and community interactions
16–21 years: thinking skills extend	◆ plans for future: considers ideas and possibilities ◆ emotional and social maturity: independence and coping skills
20–30 years: frontal lobes refine	◆ formal reasoning: high level of thinking, reflection and insight ◆ emotional refinement: altruism, love, understanding, compassion ◆ fine motor skills: develops and sustains intricate manual activities
30 years onwards: further refinements of physical and mental abilities	◆ hands and face: greater finger and face agility for improved expressive powers ◆ experience brings perspective, understanding and wisdom

TASK: What strikes you about the pattern of development shown in the table? Can you find examples of educational practice that ignore significant brain growth periods? Reflect on brain growth in relation to your school experience.

1 The cerebellum (hind brain)

The hind brain includes the cerebellum and brain stem, and is the oldest brain part, evolutionarily speaking. It develops from conception through to 15 months. It monitors the outer world through the senses (vision, hearing, feeling, touch, sense of position in space, smell, taste) and activates the body to respond to survival needs. The Thomas and Chess study (1977) discovered that adult competency stems from three factors during childhood:

◆ rich sensory experiences that build strong mental images

◆ freedom to explore safely

◆ adults who respond fully when children ask questions.

'Hands-on' sensory experience remains the basis for knowledge building all through life but in many schools the amount of active learning children experience has reduced in recent decades because of curriculum demands. Many educational practices derive from the assumption that students learn if given knowledge in spoken monologue or written two-dimensional form. Formal learning relies on verbal and written explanations. But you only have to see the glazed, locked eyes of students in class to know that this approach needs challenging!

Learning is experience. Everything else is just information.

Albert Einstein

Words are bits of data, and a poor substitute for real hands-on learning. Without active experience our images are distorted. You cannot cook a wonderful meal just by reading the cookery book – it is *making* the dish that really teaches you how to cook. 'Know that' is only useful up to a point; 'know how' is the real experience of learning something.

Think about how you can make your activities with children as practical as possible. When I headed an undergraduate medical sciences strand, the anatomy lecturer started voice structure lectures by getting student pairs to make a paper larynx. This caught their imagination and helped understanding of the complex components and their nerve structures by engaging the students in talk with one another. This was very different from my own undergraduate experience of trying to fathom the subject from *Gray's Anatomy* and the professor's words!

2 The limbic brain

At about 15 months of age, the limbic system adds emotion to the base patterns for sensory input and motor function. By five years, a child connects reason (from the cerebrum) with emotions, and by eight adds insight (from frontal lobes) to refine thought. The intricate wiring of the limbic system shows that in order to remember and learn there must be strong input from the senses, a personal and emotional connection, plus movement. This strongly supports experience-based learning.

Gelernter (1994) makes the point that emotions are not a form of thought, or an additional way to think, but are fundamental to thinking. Emotions, adding to the pain or pleasure of learning, are tied to *body states*, so we think with our brains *and* bodies. Emotional development is responsible for our ability to absorb rules, values and wisdom and without these intelligences we can do little with our learning. Goleman's popular book *Emotional Intelligence* (1996) has been influential in drawing our attention to this aspect of learning (see page 42).

The implications of these insights are enormous, especially to education. Our emotions mediate situations. Curriculum demands encourage us to deliver knowledge in separate subject areas in an unemotional and unsociable environment. The connections to students' own personal concerns are often remote. Teachers complain of being disciplinarians rather than educators as they clamp down on student emotional and social interactions. In many countries outside the UK, children do not start formal learning until age 6–7 and have a school day that comprises a long morning, giving them opportunities to develop their own interests as well as form links with the wider community during the afternoons. Childcare and parental work patterns in the UK make this difficult to establish, but we should give the issues serious thought and seek reasonable changes.

3 The cerebrum and cortex

The cerebrum and cortex comprise the largest brain structure. Put your hands together in loose fists with thumbs pointing downwards to get an idea of its size. Covering the cerebrum, like the peel of an orange, is the convoluted cortex, which is 2–5 mm thick. It contains 20 billion nerve cells, using 0.85 litres of blood each minute and burning 400 calories a day. An estimated quadrillion (a million billion) brain cell connections carry out all complex functions. Merzenich (1995) observed that whenever we engage in new behaviour the brain remodels itself. It retains this capacity throughout life as long as body and mind remain active. Even after brain damage, rewiring is possible to compensate for lost pathways. The harder we use the brain the more nerve connections are created.

The two squashy left and right cerebral hemispheres, comprising the cerebrum, lie over the small cerebellum, and only developed 100,000 years ago when human language began to develop. There are four lobes:

① **frontal** lobe (sequential movements including thoughts into speech)

② **parietal** lobe (sensation and past experiences)

③ **temporal** lobe (interpretation)

④ **occipital** lobe (visual interpretation and association).

There is an *incoming* area (sensory cortex) and an *outgoing* area (motor cortex). The four lobes accept external information from the opposite side of the body. Information from the *left* ear goes into the *right* temporal lobe for interpretation, while the *right* hand is controlled by the *left* motor cortex. All sensory–motor functions on the right side of the body are controlled by the left hemisphere and on the left the reverse usually occurs, although some people are transposed with at least part of the right-brain controlling the right side of the body and vice versa. The fact that some people use their right hand for writing and others their left is proof of brain differences. Knowledge is integrated, organized and reorganized through a bridge connecting both hemispheres, called the corpus callosum, so new experiences can be understood in the light of past memories.

What happens when children learn?

Children form *images* from sensory experience in the form of movements, feelings, tones, words, shapes and colours. The nerve networks connect these up from various parts of the brain. Movement patterns and emotional experiences are stored in the limbic system, tones and words in the temporal and frontal lobes, whereas shape and colour are held in the occipital lobes.

When we hear the word 'bus', all our experiences of it are immediately available as images. We might picture a large, noisy, smelly, dangerous, heavy, brightly coloured, large-wheeled vehicle, recalling memories of riding in buses with feelings of fright or fervour and love or hate emotions about them. Do you remember the nursery song 'The wheels on the bus go round and round', which children accompany with circular arm movements? Does this conjure up pictures in your mind? Using stored images in our memory, we make sense of new learning and come up with fresh ideas. In this way we build concepts of the world and the greater our experiences the richer these ideas are in our minds.

How can you help this learning?

When children hear or read something, their brains actively convert words into existing images for comprehension. If you cannot achieve these images it is difficult to understand. Imagery is vital to thinking and understanding and is strengthened through drama, role play and imaginary experiences.

Encourage children to close their eyes for 30 seconds and make a picture on an imaginary screen above their eyes. This is an excellent way of helping visualization and tapping into their emotional feelings. They will create dark, sharp, angry images such as animals in cages, if they are disturbed, and light, bright, happy ones, such as playing on the beach, if they are mentally stable. This is a useful way to take a child's 'emotional temperature' and assess working potential.

Asking children to talk about their mental images brings together activity in both sides of the brain. It is thought that the left-brain is largely responsible for verbalizing and the right-brain for visualizing (Bell, 1991). Both aspects of processing are needed for comprehension.

TASK: Ask students to visualize ideas and describe their pictures to stimulate both thinking and language. Get students to imagine a person, place or object that is part of the lesson content and talk about it to others.

Comment

Motor skills depend on muscle and bone growth, and a child's unique rate of body and brain development may have profound influences on self-image and confidence. Physical growth sets limits on mental development. A child cannot do what the body is not developed to do, and we are foolish if we expect otherwise. Physical readiness does not guarantee learning but is a necessary condition. Research suggests that children need opportunities to practise their emerging physical skills and we must reflect on whether our present educational system gives them sufficient opportunity. Obesity is growing in children as they spend more time sitting in front of a television than exercising their bodies (Sage, 2000b). 'Fat Camps' are now part of the range of holiday activities on offer. The problem of child obesity is exacerbated by huge media coverage of child abductions, which encourages parents to keep children indoors and less active while snacking on crisps, cola and chocolate.

◆ Mental development

Perception, thinking and language are the mental activities of foremost importance in learning.

Perception

Perception is the meaning we attribute to the messages that reach our brains from senses. School emphasizes information that we see and hear, and – to a lesser extent – that we touch and feel.

Total visual acuity is not reached until about age ten, but younger children have adequate sight for their needs. However, the fovea of the eye, dealing with two-dimensional material such as pictures and print, is not fully developed until after eight years of age. This has consequences for reading. Much pressure is put upon children reading nowadays and Hunter-Carsch (1999) has mentioned high levels of visual stress among students. It is perhaps significant that the ten countries in the world with the top levels of student achievement all start their children's schooling two years later than is the case in Britain. If children are ready to learn, they are not exposed to damaging experiences of failure.

Hearing appears to improve steadily until adolescence; older children can hear and discriminate more high and low tones, soft and loud sounds and sound levels not well discriminated by younger ones. Diorio and co-workers (1993) have shown high levels of stress hormones such as adrenaline and cortisol in very young children, which pass through the placenta from mother to child. These interfere with hearing development and are correlated with decreased learning and memory and increased attention problems. Levinson (1988) discovered that over 90 per cent of children with learning difficulties had ear infections as infants. This means large numbers of children miss hearing complex tones and are at risk of experiencing spoken and written language difficulties.

With regard to hearing and vision, there is research to suggest that young children of about three years of age are more sensitive to contrasts and contours than older ones. Later, the child probably focuses more on objects, their uses and meanings, and less on auditory and visual contours.

Young children are not able to discriminate the location of touch like older ones (Sage, 1990). A standard way to measure this is to touch a child in two places at once. Younger children often only report one touch while older ones are reliable in spotting both and errors are rare. It appears that there is not equal sensitivity over the bodies of young children.

Perceptual constancy, object concept and identity

A collection of skills called constancies, concepts and identities are vital to the learning process and develop within the first three years of life. When someone walks away from you, the image of that person becomes smaller on the retina of the eye but you perceive him as remaining the same size. This demonstrates *size constancy*. A skill needed for this is depth perception. Next time you are in an aeroplane, take a look at things on the ground. People and cars look like midgets and toys. As there is no reliable way to estimate distance, size constancy cannot be maintained. You know their real size but they look smaller. Ability to recognize that shapes are the same even though you see them from a different angle, and that colours are the same even though the amount of light or shadow may change, are other forms of constancy. Children have to learn their own constancy and continuity.

In addition to constancy, two facets of object concepts are learned. First, children must understand that an object exists even when they cannot see or feel it, as when someone goes from the room or a toy is put away. This is known as object permanence. Finally, a child must realize that objects retain their individual identity from one encounter to the next. When someone disappears and then returns they are the same person. This understanding is known as *object identity*; animate (living) objects appear to be recognized as having object identity before inanimate ones (Bell, 1970). This illustrates the intricate interconnections between the development of perception and of relationships between people. Positive, responsive relationships with others influence further contacts in which the child engages. Supporting children who have not developed positive relationships takes time, patience and a calm approach and it often falls to the teaching assistant, learning mentor or counsellor to cope with these difficult issues.

Attention

A great deal of research has been devoted to the pattern of attention. What are the child's preferences? How does she attend? Things that are moderately novel are attended to most, because the child has to assimilate new to old (Piaget, 1964). Initially, attention is for the single figure or parts of a picture or object; from age two months, a process of de-centring occurs, whereby the child shows less concentrated focus on single objects. Kagan (1971) points out that rules change as children get older because they are able to interpret differences and form hypotheses. Underlying attention is the idea of expectation. Cooper and co-workers (1978) suggest six stages of attention control, useful for teaching:

1–2 years   **distractible**: momentary attention

2–3 years   **concentrates for a time**: on task of his own choice

3–4 years **attention for one input only**: can't listen if involved in task; need adult to set attention focus

4–5 years **attention still for one input**: can attend under his own control

5–6 years **attention for two inputs**: can assimilate information while engaged in tasks

6–7 years **integrated attention**: established and maintained.

Gibson (1969) suggests that optimization of attention is guided by four principles:

① captured to voluntary: attention 'captured' by things, which later becomes voluntary

② unsystematic to systematic search: focus on bits only and later the whole

③ broad to selective: from the whole can select parts

④ inability to ignore irrelevancies to ability to do so: shuts out unwanted information.

The trend is towards more voluntary attention control as the child develops, but many entering school have not achieved Cooper's 'integrated attention' or Gibson's third and fourth dimension, so learning is slowed. It is important not to expect task control above the child's level of development, as this results in frustration and misery for both student and teacher.

TASK: Use the Cooper or Gibson guide to work out a child's attention level and then try to encourage progression to the next stage using time targets (get the child to try attending for one minute, then for two, and so on).

Differences in perceptual development

Although there is variation in the rate at which perceptual skills are acquired, generally the child's chronological age is the best predictor. There are, however, interesting differences in style and preference. Kagan (1965) suggested that children differ in 'conceptual tempo'. Some, confronted with something new, pause and examine it carefully and quietly, while others become excited and active and do not observe it for as long. This reflective/impulsive style appears stable and the reflective child has an easier time learning to read. Witkin and co-workers (1962) observed the same phenomena with older children and adults. This demonstrates the effect of personality dispositions on development.

More of the child's perceptual skills are present at birth than was previously thought, but the role of experience and learning cannot be underestimated. There are few consistent sex differences in perception, but girls appear to be less tolerant of pain and more sensitive to taste. No social class differences have been found but older children from poorer backgrounds are more likely to be impulsive in their visual scanning of information and less successful learners.

Thinking

There are two major strands to research on thinking:

1. intelligence testing
2. stages of development and learning strategies.

Intelligence testing

Two Frenchmen, Binet and Simon (1916), published the first intelligence tests in 1905 to predict school success. The rationale was that people differ in brightness or ability and this could be measured on verbal and non-verbal tests. The intelligence quotient (IQ) is based on a comparison of actual age (chronological age) with mental age. The formula is:

$$(\text{mental age} \div \text{chronological age}) \times 100 = IQ$$

A child with the chronological age of five who solves all the problems for five and six year olds, but nothing above this level, has an IQ of 120:

$$(6 \div 5) \times 100 = 120$$

A child of six with a mental age of four would have an IQ of 67:

$$(4 \div 6) \times 100 = 67$$

Such tests measure a limited number of thinking skills in an arbitrary fashion and do not indicate where the person is in terms of development, as already discussed (pages 32 and 71–74). However, they tell us something about performance in comparison to peers and predict school success with some reliability.

Test scores are influenced by the child's heredity, although it is not clear which factors most affect performance. Environment plays a major role. While a child inherits a range of potential abilities, where he will actually function within that range depends on the kind of environment he grows up in. Those offering secure, happy experiences and positive encouragement facilitate maximum growth, but others are depressing, limited and uninspiring, which inhibit development.

Research has shown that children from middle-class families, who value learning, score higher on standard tests. Regardless of social class, parents who provide appropriate play experiences, interact with their child, offer love and support, and expect success tend to have children who score well on tests. Interventions, such as all-day enriched day care from infancy, have positive effects on scores. Children with high scores are likely to be those who explore and experiment and are independent and assertive. They are often first-born children who receive undivided adult attention. There are no significant sex differences, although males score higher in spatial ability and mathematical reasoning, whereas females test better on verbal reasoning and vocabulary tests. Test scores are strongly influenced by specific situations such as health and conditions of testing.

Comment

Many people feel uneasy about assigning a number to a child's performance. Traditional tests favour those who have good language abilities, but Gardner's (1993) multiple intelligences theory (logical–mathematical, linguistic, visual spatial, bodily-kinesthetic, musical, interpersonal and intrapersonal) gives value to a wider range, including the skill of communicating well with others. Nevertheless, the intelligence test movement has demonstrated the effects of secure, supportive, stimulating learning environments and allowed standard comparisons between performances. Tests can be a useful part of a larger assessment scheme, providing quantitative evidence to judge ability.

Thinking development

The sequence of development, which appears in general outline to be the same for all children, can be broken down into four periods or stages. Piaget and Inhelder (1969), Bruner and co-workers (1966) and Vygotsky (1962) are influential psychologists in the child development field.

Stages in thinking development						
Stage	Age (years)	Names given to stage			Description	Notes
		Piaget	Bruner	Vygotsky		
1	0–2	Sensori-motor	Enactive	Pre-language	Interactions are sensory and active: seeing, hearing, reaching, touching, grasping, sucking. Reflexes and chance govern exploration, with movements not intended or planned.	◆ Movement from reflexive to intentional behaviour. ◆ No internal representation of the world.
2	2–6	Pre-operational	Iconic	Represent-ational	Begins to represent objects/events in words but reasoning is limited to own desires (egocentric/self-centred). At 6, the child starts to de-centre and think beyond himself.	◆ Thinking egocentric. ◆ Reasoning less tied to specific experience. ◆ Classifies objects and concepts.
3	6–11	Concrete operations	Symbolic	Creative Language	Manipulates representations as in ordering events. Says what he sees (rehearsal) to aid memory.	◆ Makes complex classifications. ◆ Performs operations like addition, subtraction and ordering on actual experience/objects.
4	11+	Formal operations	–	–	Uses complex mental operations on things that he has experienced and searches systematically for solutions to problems.	◆ Shifts from inductive (reasoning from facts) to deductive (reasoning from principles): 'If all men are equal, then you and I must be equal.' ◆ Systematic in exploration and search. ◆ Thinks about thinking.

Comment

This theory of thinking development is influential, but there are criticisms. Children do not all develop at the same rate and this is not addressed. They are not at a given 'stage' on every task or in every situation, which suggests some inconsistency in the stages. Some ages for activities may not be accurate. Borke (1975) reports that three to four year olds are less egocentric (self-centred) than the theory outlined above maintains. Nevertheless, there is general support for a gradual progression of thinking through a fixed sequence of skills and discoveries. In those over the age of three, there is evidence that middle-class children are a year or two more advanced than others from poorer environments. Analyses of mother–child interactions show that aspects of early stimulation, such as the variety and complexity of toys and the amount the child is talked with and stimulated, may hasten or retard mental development. No sex differences in rate of progress have been consistently found (Yarrow and co-workers, 1972).

 TASK: Think of a child you are involved with and consider her development against the appropriate stage in the table opposite. How does the child's performance fit? Is this below or above what would be expected according to actual age?

Language and communication

Learning and teaching is a communicative experience in which information is constantly being exchanged between participants. There are two main perspectives on communication:

1. component model: a process whereby a sender directs a message through a medium or channel to a receiver, with some effect

2. context model: a social activity where people create and exchange meanings in response to the reality they experience.

In education, stronger emphasis is placed on the component model.

Communication is a non-stop activity, as even in sleep our minds rearrange memories in the shape of dream images. While awake we absorb and give out information, both deliberately and unconsciously. We may say one thing and signal another meaning in our gestures or facial expressions – for example, we might say a child's work is good, with a grimace on our face, because we really think it is bad but feel we ought to be positive.

It is important to note that students may have adequate speech and language structure but still not be able to use it for effective communication, thinking, social interaction and personal control. In schools, spoken and written words are the important medium. Consider the conversation shown overleaf between a teacher and six-year-old Mark. What patterns can you detect?

Teacher:	(*teaching a lesson on conservation, using two balls of modelling clay*) Mark, hold these two balls and tell me whether there is the same amount of clay in each.
Mark:	Yeh.
Teacher :	Now, I'm going to change one of the balls into a sausage shape, like this. (*Shapes one of the balls into a sausage shape in front of Mark.*) Is there the same amount of clay in both balls?
Mark:	Um, umm. (*Nodding his head*)
Teacher:	If you put it back into the ball, it would be the same.
Mark:	It would be the same. (**imitation**)
Teacher:	It would be the same but is longer and thinner, but I haven't added or taken any away so it must be the same amount. (**reinforcement**)
Mark:	It's big around but is the same.
Teacher:	The ball is bigger around but shorter than the sausage, which is longer and thinner. They are different in shape but not in amount. (**expansion**)

Did you notice the following three patterns?

❶ **Expansions**: instances in which the adult repeats what the child has just said, expanding it into a complete, adult, grammatical sentence.

❷ **Imitations**: instances in which the child imitates what the adult has just said either exactly or with some simplification, so that his sentence is less complex.

❸ **Reinforcement**: responses by the adult to the form of the child's answer.

During conversations, adults are not only giving children information, but also helping them to structure their ideas through words. Language is, therefore, central to human experience, being a key vehicle for thought and social contact. Human beings are mutually dependent and effective communication between them requires that:

◆ they know the forms of language they share; how words sound, combine and are used and arranged in sentences (competence in phonology, grammar and syntax)

◆ they are able to bring together verbal and non-verbal messages to understand the communication of others, and use verbal and non-verbal modes to convey their own meaning (competence in information processing and production plus semantics)

◆ they understand and use the conventions that determine how people communicate with each other and appreciate each other's intention (competence in pragmatics)

◆ they are able to vary their style (register) of communication to suit the needs of different listeners, and understand the styles used by others in both dialogues (short exchanges) and monologues (long narratives) (competence in conversation moves and narrative thinking)

◆ they understand how language and communication use varies within different social contexts (competence in socio-linguistics).

Children may have problems mastering some or all of these areas of competence, some of which are linguistic and others cognitive and social. Often difficulties are not detected, because most of us are ineffective communicators with limited understanding of this very dynamic and complex process. Thus, if students function adequately in short dialogues, we assume that they can do so in the monologue situations of a classroom, where the teacher talks for most of the time and students have to put together great chunks of information from a variety of sources to make meaning. That many children struggle with this should come as no surprise, when you appreciate the leap they have to make between short and long exchanges.

Traditionally, most attention has been given to three types of competence:

◆ phonology (sound system)

◆ grammar (word functions – nouns, verbs and so on)

◆ syntax (word arrangements – subject–verb–object, plus phrase and clause structure).

This emphasis on language has diverted attention away from narrative structure, the way that meaning is conveyed. Teachers quickly pick up distorted sounds and limited vocabulary, but problems with narrative are often put down to poor listening and attention. A look at the stages involved in processing a sentence will help to illustrate this issue. For example, let us consider the processing of the sentence 'The cat is on the table':

1 **sound processing**: sound waves are transmitted into a neural spectrum

2 **extraction of phonetic features**: voice, friction, nasality and so on

3 **analysis of the sound sequence**: consonant–vowel patterns

4 **recognition of the sound sequence**: the series of six words

5 **association of words with sound, sight, feeling images**: for example, 'cat' = soft, furry, purrs, and so on

6 **recognition of the word structure**: subject (noun phrase – 'the cat'; verb – 'is'), object (object phrase – 'on the table')

7 **representation of the proposition** (probably in pictorial form): theme – cat located on a table

8 **mental operation to infer and evaluate the information**: that is, working out the reason why the cat is on the table as a step towards understanding

9 **interpretation of the meaning from context clues and general knowledge**: that is, bringing together all the available information from the surrounding context for understanding; in this case, the cat was on the table with his paw in the goldfish bowl!

The issue is that the sentence itself conveys very little on its own and can only have meaning within a specific context. The cat on the table, in the sentence above, may be real or ornamental and be in that location to gobble the goldfish or perhaps to be groomed. Reference to context, with ability to use experience, knowledge and available clues to refer, infer and cohere the meaning are the mental operations that integrate with linguistic knowledge to produce communication. Language structure thus merges with narrative structure to achieve meaning.

It is clear that putting together teacher monologues is impossible without a well-developed ability to analyse, synthesize and evaluate information – the skills that are generally weak in both children and adults, because of a lack of opportunities to develop talk and thinking in our modern, hurried lives (Sage, 2000b).

Students experience problems with communication because they have not developed their higher thinking processes, but also because the conventions of communication use at home are very different to those of school. At home, it is children who do the talking and the questioning, and the adults who should listen and respond; but in school the process is reversed. Unless experienced in the variety of social conventions that operate in different contexts, children are likely to find school language a hindrance rather than a help to learning.

Communicative competence is more important than linguistic competence in terms of making relationships and understanding what is going on. Guy, aged 12, illustrates the point. His teacher asks if he intends to go on the forthcoming school trip to the Science Museum; Guy replies with a statement about his Mum's recent spell in hospital.

Teacher: Guy, are you going on the Year 9 Science trip on Friday?

Guy: Mum's been in the National Heart Hospital. She's had an operation on a valve. It's been a long job. We still don't know when she's coming home. I've been to see her every night from school. My Dad picks me up and we go and get my Nan and then we're off. We always have a fish-and-chip supper on the way back.

Guy's sentences are produced with accurate pronunciation, syntax and intonation, but he never looks at the listener; he talks at length, but without apparent relevance to the context. Guy's teacher describes him as a poor listener, but he displays a higher order problem in communication. This performance would be acceptable for a three year old but not for someone in secondary school.

How do children develop language?

There are several theories about language development, which are worth examining as many of our support strategies are based on them.

1   **Imitation**: The most obvious theory is that language results from the child's imitation of adults. However, children's language is unique and creative from the beginning and they do more reducing of what they hear than straight imitating. Since so much of what children hear is imperfect language, the imitation theory cannot be a complete explanation, but there is no doubt that it plays a part, especially in early stages when infants often repeat what they hear.

2   **Reinforcement**: The second alternative is that children are shaped into language by some reinforcement pattern. Although reinforcement principles apply to aspects of language, particularly pronunciation, there is no evidence that it is systematically applied to all grammar learning.

3 **Analysis**: A third alternative places emphasis on ability to analyse adult language patterns and extract rules from them, which children copy and simplify for their own use. There must be some truth in this idea, because when you tell a child a story to be retold, they do so in a simplified way to match their level of thinking and language. Such analyses, however, are well beyond the abilities of infants.

4 **Language acquisition device**: There has been much interest in the idea that children are born with a tendency to sort and learn rules for language transformations. Chomsky (1965) proposed that sentences have an essential meaning (deep structure) and this is transformed by rules into a specific sentence (surface structure). For example, supposing the deep structure is 'Freya likes pears'; transformational rules can turn this into a question ('Does Freya like pears?'), or passive question ('Are pears liked by Freya?'), and so on. This is an enormously complex theory, but it makes sense that children have some inbuilt system for dealing with the language that they hear.

No one alternative provides a comprehensive theory of language development, accounting for all that is observed or dealing adequately with word meaning. There is agreement, however, that there is a biological underpinning to language learning, and a structure for sound and sentence development, which is outlined below and overleaf.

Development of the sound system of English			
Age (years)	Lip	Tongue (front)	Tongue (back)
0–1	first words with much individual variation		
1–2	p b m w	t d n	
2–2.5	p b m w	t d n	k g ng h
2.5–3.5	p b m f w	t d n s y l	k g ng h
3.5–4.5	p b m f v w	t d n s z y l	k g ng sh ch j h
4.5+	p b m f v w	t d n s z y l	k g ng sh ch j h
5–6	p b m f v w th	t d n s z y l r	k g ng sh ch j h
6–7	blends: tw tr dr pl str shr spl		

You will find that some children have not acquired the sound system by seven years and if this is the case there will be problems acquiring word-building skills for reading and spelling.

Development of word patterns (syntax)		
Age (years)	Feature	Example
1–2	Uses two-word combinations. Has no sense of word order.	'Car nice' 'Biscuit want'
2–3	Uses three-word combinations. Talks about the present only.	'He lose shoe' 'Where lady go?' 'Give Mummy cup'
3–4	Uses four-word combinations. Uses statements, questions, comments. Associates ideas: for example, knife and fork. Many words left out in a sequence.	'Luke kicking ball now'
4–5	Uses co-ordinating words (and, but, so) and connectives (because, where). Uses five attributes to describe (shape, name, colour, size, feel).	'I like chocs but I don't like spinach.' 'Round ball. It's blue, big and squashy.'
5–6	Uses language beyond the immediate situation. Orders ideas in some way.	Q. 'If baby falls what does Mummy do?' A. 'She picks him up and puts a plaster on if he is hurt.'
6–7	Tells back information with about half the details correct. Uses features to connect up talk (then, after, before, however). Replays events in the past – a holiday or weekend.	

TASK: Can you think of a child that you know in the 1–7 age range? Does she match up with the language development outlined above?

Acquiring the ability to form sounds and sentences does not mean that a child can use them. In order to cope with the large amount of talk that happens in school a child must have the following conversational moves (Sage, 2000b). The student must be able to:

1 answer a **closed question** ('what'/'who'/'when'/'where') demanding a specific response

2 contribute an idea (even if not entirely appropriate) showing **turn taking** ability

3 listen and respond, showing **maintenance** moves such as eye contact for 75 per cent of the time, smiling, nodding, and so on

4 answer an **open question** ('how'/'why') demanding an explanation

5 **initiate a new idea** in conversation that fits in with the topic under discussion.

If all moves are in place, this indicates an ability to follow either a spoken or written narrative. Listening (move 3) with a forward posture and maintained eye contact suggests concentration and co-operation in exchanges. If attention wanders, it is a sign that the listener is bored or finds the information presented in an unhelpful way or above their level of discourse ability. Answering open questions (move 4) demands higher level thinking ability to express cause and effect and link events. (For example, 'Baljit, why are you drinking milk?' 'Because I like it better than orange.') This linking of events clearly is the base for putting together information in talk or text. Initiating a new idea (move 5) shows ability to connect ideas logically within the overall theme. It demands an overview of the situation and an understanding of the parts that fit together and make a whole (top-down and bottom-up processing).

These conversational moves require the thinking skills of analysis, synthesis and evaluation mentioned in Chapter 4 in Bloom's taxonomy (page 73). Do not assume that children have these moves on starting school. Many secondary students have problems with 'why' and 'how' questions and cannot follow the lesson narrative easily, make explanations or give instructions. Skills and Enterprise Briefings suggest that communication is the weakest ability in the workplace (Mason, 1996). My research has suggested that even talented and gifted students have difficulties with narrative structure, confirmed by Wilde (2004) in her work with such children on the Communication Opportunity Group Scheme.

Comment

The rate of language and communication development differs considerably from one child to the next, and I have seen many students in secondary schools who communicate only at the level of a five year old. They can chat, but have problems following the connected discourse of instruction and explanation and making a coherent response. Language development has occurred but narrative thinking has fallen behind, probably in a large number of cases because of restricted opportunities to use language in a variety of ways. Narrative also has a developmental structure (Sage, 2000b):

1. **Record**: produce ideas
2. **Recite**: order ideas in a limited way but not in a time sequence
3. **Refer**: compare ideas
4. **Replay**: sequence ideas in time
5. **Recount**: explain ideas (Why? How?)
6. **Report**: discuss ideas – giving an opinion
7. **Relate**: tell a story with setting, events, actions, reactions.

This is a guide to how we develop our ability to deal with a number of ideas, and it is not difficult to understand the close relation between narrative ability and thinking. Bruner and co-workers (1966) suggest that language and thought are separate until about the age of six. They then come together as an aid to memory, problem solving and analysis. Dale (1976) suggests that mastering the linguistic system is not the same thing as putting it to work. Language is not used for many functions – memory, classification, and inner speech – until a point in development considerably later than the essential mastery of structure. Putting language to work is what developing narrative is about but school puts a brake on talk and does not easily facilitate development of thinking and expression.

How can you help?

Use the guides to sound, sentence and narrative structure to work out where your students fall on the developmental continuum. Try to encourage them to progress to the level above by modelling this yourself so students hear the structures, but do not put pressure on them to achieve these until they spontaneously do so.

For example, if a child has developed all the sounds up to the 5 year stage but is not at the 5–6 year level pronouncing 'th' and 'r' correctly, try to use words with these sounds in them so the child has plenty of opportunity to hear them, but do not ask for these words to be repeated back to you until the child wants to do so.

Similarly, with sentences, if a child is using language to talk about the past and future, he should be encouraged to hear stories and tell them back.

With regard to narrative, the test is to see if a child can express a number of things about an object. This is the beginning of narrative expression. See where the child is on the development guide and then stimulate the next level by modelling.

◆ Emotional development

Life is a comedy for those who think and a tragedy for those who feel.

Horace Walpole

> Mrs Brown was telling Greg off for kicking Kirsty in the playground. 'I don't care!' he shouted angrily, his eyes momentarily filling with tears.

Greg is showing with his tears that his 'heart' is sad even if his 'head' is saying words to the contrary. These two minds, the emotional and rational, operate in tight harmony for the most part. Feelings are essential to thought, and vice versa. When passions surge, however, the balance tips and the emotional mind takes the upper hand with the cortex deferring to the limbic system (see pages 81 and 83). The connections between the limbic structures and the cerebral cortex, through a small almond-shaped part called the amygdala, strike a balance between head and heart, thought and feeling. An important aspect of learning is developing the ability to deal with your emotions – and this can be a painful business.

Of concern to teachers is the child's aggression and attachment (dependency). The earliest patterns of interactions between carer and infant seem to take the form of a kind of dance in which the child signals with eye contact, smiles and chuckles, and the adult responds. Attachment to the child may be affected by the ability of the pair to achieve satisfactory communication with one another. Communication, therefore, is an essential base for emotional development and many researchers have looked at the connection between this development and behaviour (Cohen, 1996).

There are clear sequences in the development of attachments, going from diffuse to single and then to multiple attachments (Ainsworth, 1973). In older children there is a shift away from dependent behaviours such as clinging, holding and touching, towards mature forms such as seeking attention and approval. Children differ in the strength and quality of their early attachments and the speed in which they pass from immature to mature forms of dependency. Consistency in dependent behaviour is more notable in females than males, and is the reason why there are more boys in school with emotional and behaviour problems. Individual differences are partly determined by care practices although the child's temperament (discussed earlier) may be influential. Among older children the degree of dependency seems to be jointly determined by the amount of reward and punishment that adults provide in response to the child's bids for dependency.

Developmental trends in aggressive behaviour are less clear than for attachment, but they suggest a shift from physical to verbal aggression as the child gets older (Goodenough, 1931). Individual differences appear marked, with boys showing more physical aggression (probably because of their strength and hormones) at all ages. Consistency in aggression through life is more apparent in males than females. There is reason to suppose that the baby comes equipped with a link between frustration and aggression, as this is such a common response in all children. Other responses to frustration can be learned. Some child-rearing practices have been consistently linked with high levels of aggression and these include rejection, high levels of physical punishment, and a combination of permissiveness and punishment. The context for emotional development is vital and Erikson (1963) highlights this in his stages of emotional maturity:

1. **early infancy**: trust versus mistrust
2. **late infancy**: autonomy versus shame and doubt
3. **early childhood**: initiative versus guilt
4. **middle childhood**: competence versus inferiority
5. **adolescence**: identity versus role confusion
6. **early adulthood**: intimacy versus isolation
7. **middle adulthood**: production versus stagnation
8. **late adulthood**: self-acceptance versus despair.

The stages are based on a series of contrasts. As the child, adolescent, young and old adult experience life they develop positive or negative concepts of themselves in relation to what happens and what is communicated to them. For example, if the young infant sets up good communicative relationships with others he will learn *trust*, but if they are bad, *mistrust* occurs. Erikson proposes a growth pattern of constructs, which slot into other learning. When the child is in school and able to compare his performance against others, he starts to grasp an idea of his competence in relation to them. If he sees himself doing worse than his peers, feelings of inferiority will be experienced and learned. Sage (2003) argues that these abstract concepts, based on fundamental notions of good and bad, are the way a child analyses the world. All early experiences, such as feeding and care, generate good or bad feelings for the child. These become the base measure for judging succeeding events.

Clearly, the concept of 'self' that emerges from experiences includes both the child's view of herself (self-concept), her body and abilities (self-image) and her degree of self-esteem (value for self). The earliest stage is the discovery that she is separate from others, constant and continuous. By the age of two the child has learned her name and by three has achieved a measure of autonomy as a result of developing physical, mental, social and emotional skills. At four, the child shows possessiveness about her space and things and by five to six can verbalize her thoughts and emotions and form positive or negative judgements about herself. Meadows (1993) reminds us, however, that children cannot be relied on to express their feelings accurately, as it takes many years to identify and communicate these. Also, many children appear to have problems with communicating effectively in formal contexts. Children with low esteem are anxious and have more difficulties coping with school. Those with high esteem have their achievements valued and praised, experiencing a warm relationship with clear communication and limits set on behaviour (Merry, 1998). Men are more confident in new tasks, but this may well change as women take on more leading roles in society.

How can we support emotional development?

In schools, we are learning to take a child's emotions more seriously and terms like 'emotional literacy' allude to the importance of attending to the feelings of students. Research on emotional development and self-concept suggests that the communicative relationship between the child and others is the key to successful learning. In our relationships with others we learn what they think of us and, even if this is not communicated in words, it most definitely will be demonstrated in actions such as tone of voice, facial expressions and gestures. Wragg (1994) reminds us that in schools, four out of five comments to children are negative; we can make a conscious effort to reverse this and ensure that feedback is largely positive.

◆ Social development

No man is an island, entire of itself.

John Donne

Children are born into a society of others, and socializing them into its norms is a major task. There are five theories, outlined opposite. None of them accounts adequately for developmental patterns and individual differences, but they are useful reference points for our attitudes and views.

Social development theories	
The ethological theory (Bowlby, 1969)	This emphasizes inborn, instinctive patterns of interaction. The child provokes care by cries and movements and prolongs it with smiles and chuckles. With development, the instinctive patterns come under the child's control. Attention is focused on the patterns of interaction that the child appears naturally to bring with him into the world.
The psychoanalytic approach 1 (Freud, 1960)	This concentrates on instinctive behaviour of self-preservation, with focus on sexual development. At each stage, sexual energy (libido) is invested in a specific part of the body (erogenous zone) and the maturational shift is triggered by changes in sensitivity of the different regions. The stages are: **0–1 years**: oral (mouth) **1–3 years**: anal (bottom) **3–5 years**: phallic (genitals) **5–12 years**: latency (resting period with own sex relationships) **12–18 years**: genital (sexual energy) The important event in the phallic stage is the Oedipal conflict, in which a boy becomes aware of his mother as a sex object and competes with his father. The conflict is resolved when he identifies with father and represses feelings for mother. For girls, the conflict is different as the original attachment is to mother with a shift to father. For this theory, the broad outline of the development of attachments is accepted, but not the dynamics of the process.
The psychoanalytic approach 2 (Erikson, 1963)	This focuses on changes in the child's motor and cognitive skills and the impact these have on interactions. The eight stages are described on page 99. Erikson's theory has been influential because it brings together mental and personality development and accounts for individual differences in interactions.
Social learning theories (Bandura, 1973)	These emphasize that the child's way of interacting with others is learned. Attachment is based on having needs met repeatedly with good things, so that the child begins to see the people who provide them as positive. Obviously, a child's response is influenced by others' responses to her. Children do learn in ways that please adults and from observing models.
Cognitive-developmental theories (Kohlberg, 1966)	The essential tenet of this approach is that the behaviour of a child results from his mental level. Changes in attachments are seen as the result of shifts in thinking ability.

Comment

Each theory of social development offers a particular strength. The ethological theory tells us about early interaction, while social learning concepts help us to understand what happens over the childhood years. The cognitive-developmentalists point out the critical mental underpinnings to relations with others. Erikson's psychoanalytic theory combines several of these threads.

The theories do not clarify the nature of a child's social interaction at home and school. Outside class, a child has many one-to-one and small-group exchanges, which are informal in nature and not judged as right or wrong responses. In these interactions, it is usually the child who asks the questions and the adult who gives the answers. The child has an opportunity to control the exchange.

In school, the opposite occurs, with adults continually questioning and requiring 'correct' answers. Children, in class, are only allowed to talk at the teacher's direction. They are forced into a passive role and easily become anonymous within the large class group. Teaching assistants, learning mentors and counsellors have a great opportunity to work with children in one-to-one situations or small groups. They can give students some control over the exchange and help to balance the large class situation, using approaches such as the Communication Opportunity Group Scheme (Sage, 2000a). Paulo Freire (1972) describes the ideal class interaction for successful learning, which replaces the teacher as the 'sage on the stage' with a 'guide by the side'!

According to Freire, successful class interaction involves:

1 students expressing themselves so that they can hear each other's voices and opinions (even if they are just saying their names)

2 space for external input from teacher or another expert on the topic

3 dialogue in pairs, small groups or large groups (depending on size) to reflect on the input

4 students summarizing the input and reflection (in pairs or groups) and recording their summary if necessary.

This model gives greater control, in learning, to the student. If valued and practised, it produces much more able, interested and committed children, who view themselves as active participants in the process. Frequently these days, curriculum demands have made teachers' discourse the order of the day, as they monopolize class talk in order to thrash through prescribed topics. It is worth remembering that you can only really communicate effectively if there is some equality in the interaction. This is the rule outside class but not inside and many students are frustrated by it.

Roles

Traditional theories also say very little about *roles* in social interaction and how these affect the exchange. A role is a part a person plays within a given group and situation. The part requires certain kinds of behaviour, which define the person's relationship with others in the group. For example, within the family you may have the parts of oldest daughter, sister, niece and cousin. Custom gives you special responsibility as the oldest daughter – your parents view you as a pillar of strength in all family affairs and you expect to be taken into their confidence. As an older sister, you feel responsible for your younger sisters and brothers. So each of these roles in the family entitles you to certain rights, but involves obligations too. Our positions determine whether we are a leader or follower in a group and give different opportunities to learn social skills.

All the world's a stage, and all the men and women merely players; they have their exits and their entrances and one man in his time plays many parts.

William Shakespeare, As You Like It (Act 2, scene 7)

Each of us plays many roles in the course of our lives. Social scientists have attempted classifications of these parts. Basic roles depend on sex, age, position in the family and class, none of which is ours through merit. Occupational roles are largely achieved through our own merits and may include the parts children play in school. If you are viewed as physically, mentally, emotionally and socially able you are likely to be assigned leading roles, offering you greater opportunities than others demonstrating lesser abilities. Reflect on the different roles you play in different areas of your life. For example, *you* might play:

◆ **family roles** – daughter/son; sister/brother; cousin; granddaughter/grandson; aunt/uncle; and so on

◆ **social roles** – friend; acquaintance; team-mate; member of sports, drama, music group; and so on

◆ **work roles** – educator; part-time student; other part-time jobs.

In our social life, there is some choice as to which role we adopt as we take account of the situation itself, the other people and ourselves. Even so, some situations prescribe roles very clearly. For example, if your friend is in hospital, recovering from an operation, then in your visitor role you are expected to bring comfort and support and the customary grapes and flowers! What about the other person? Your role will depend on a variety of factors, and be influenced by things like age, gender, kinship, class and occupation.

In work, you will have a role to play with colleagues, children and their parents. What are your expectations and how does your educator role influence how others respond to you? Students will see teachers as authority figures, but since the role of a teaching assistant, learning mentor or counsellor is likely to be more intimate than that of a class teacher, they will view them as more like a parent, with a special, personal relationship with them. However, teaching assistants, mentors and counsellors have teaching functions that expect children to respond to them correctly, which may produce tension and stress in the relationship.

Finally, the role you choose depends on your own self-image, and at the beginning of any social encounter two people negotiate over the roles they adopt. Our relationships are more harmonious if we make clear our role and accept those played by others. If a colleague is playing the earnest expert and you persist in finding him funny then the interaction will collapse.

Your choice of role has many consequences. It affects how you dress, the way you speak and are spoken to, the kinds of rights or obligations you may expect, the sort of people you might encounter and so forth. If you regard yourself as an educated sophisticate, you will dress smartly and attractively, talk about serious ideas with others and expect to be invited to courses and lectures rather than football matches!

Understanding and diversifying our roles is an important part of our development. Children in school play many parts, not only 'learner' but also 'class star', 'fool' or 'troublemaker', and so on. Some roles may deflect from their primary one as learner. Sage (2000b) expands on this, looking at examples of children with learning problems and how their adopted role as 'poor learner' deprives them in subtle ways of many opportunities to learn. Small children play adult roles of mothers and fathers or doctors and nurses to reach some understanding of what it is like to be in these positions. Role play is an important technique in learning. To adopt an unfamiliar role demands empathy, so the player might subsequently see an antagonist such as a parent, teacher or policeman in a new light, which could help avoid conflicts.

TIP: As an educator, try to make sure children experience working in many different groups that give them opportunities to play 'leader' and 'follower' roles. Also, reverse roles in a task so that they are teaching you what they have learned and can appreciate your part in the learning with greater understanding.

◆ Review

An attempt has been made to overview the main ideas that define how processes and skills develop for learning. There are many different theories about this. All are interesting and give us opportunities to reflect more closely on a very complex process in which children bring together their physical, mental, emotional and social development as the base for their achievements. There is a rough consensus that growth is a gradual process, based on innate potential and a positive environment. Many things can interfere with this development and there are large numbers of children who arrive in schools without the foundations to learn. By considering theories, educators have the knowledge to give appropriate input to children and encourage interesting and worthwhile responses that perhaps should not be judged as 'right' or 'wrong' but as a valuable contribution to a child's learning. It is worth noting that interventions are generally based on developmental guidelines.

Main Points

- ◆ Key skills – including personal and social qualities, decision making, communication, performance, numeracy and information technology skills – are often neglected in the curriculum drive for information delivery.
- ◆ Key skills depend on physical, mental, emotional and social components of learning.
- ◆ Aspects of learning integrate to support development.
- ◆ Growth is gradual and generally thought to follow a developmental course.
- ◆ Children achieve learning at different rates due to within- and without-the-child factors.
- ◆ Learning requires good positive communication and support from adults.
- ◆ Educators have a unique opportunity to develop effective learning by giving children some control of the process and encouraging thinking and spoken communication.

Chapter Six

What approaches support inclusion?

Overview

Children need personal skills, particularly communication skills, in order to cope with social learning. Although education has traditionally espoused both academic and personal development, rigid curriculum targets have often diverted attention away from student needs and focused mainly on attainment. Shockingly, statistics suggest that many children enter school without even the necessary personal skills to interact and learn. The Critical Skills Programme and the Communication Opportunity Group Scheme help to redress the present imbalance by encouraging an altered teaching style, giving students more chances to talk, think, express feelings and share views. Such initiatives signal a move away from the teacher-dominated classroom but need the support of major policy makers and practitioners to be implemented fully. Radical solutions are essential to cope with the world of difference now apparent in our schools. To make inclusion a reality, we must enjoy the challenge of change!

◆ Introduction

Let's meet Eddy, a 14-year-old lad. He is on the side of the road, outside the village where he lives, talking to some chaps who are building a by-pass. Eddy has a list of questions he wants answered about how the road is being built. He has negotiated some time with a young surveyor and with construction experts who are laying pipes beneath the new road surface. He is fascinated to learn that one of the 22 different pipes being sited is designed for hedgehogs, allowing them a safe passage underneath the busy new highway!

Eddy's parents have taken him out of school. He spent years being depressed and miserable in a variety of different educational environments. Although a bright boy, his performance is lowered by a moderate degree of dyspraxia (see page 152). This congenital condition affects Eddy's ability to organize his thoughts and his movements. He appears slow in comparison with his peers and school was nothing short of a continual nightmare for him.

The only milieu in which Eddy appears to flourish is a Communication Opportunity Group Scheme (Sage, 2000a), which he attends for an hour each Friday evening. The scheme develops thinking and its expression in both speaking and writing. Children begin by presenting their ideas informally in conversation but then learn to structure them in situations where they have to show and tell – informing, explaining and instructing others. It is this *formal* speaking (narrative skill) which allows the shift from spoken ideas into written ones. The scheme emphasizes narrative thinking and structure over 14 goal levels, requiring core and specific competences to be achieved after 10 hours of teaching. Participants are able to choose the content for each of their five final assessment activities, so giving them an important degree of control over their learning.

For the last two years, Eddy's education has centred on the COGS goals; his project on road building was based on Goal Level 5 criteria, which required him to explain how something was made or built for the *content* section of the assessment. To complement Goal 5 activities, Eddy and two other group members wrote a play, 'Jacko and the Whacko Beans', which has been recorded by the BBC for children's radio. When Eddy was assessed recently by two psychologists from the local education authority, they were impressed by his personal skills and ability to learn, which had not been evident in what for him was the damaging environment of school.

Eddy was asked at his educational review what was important to help him learn. He came out with three things:

1 **Tools to help me learn**
   School is such a lot of speaking and listening, which I was bad at doing – I couldn't hack lessons. No one thought I needed special help because I could talk. Now I have learned to communicate clearly through COGS I have become confident, because I know how to control and cope with my learning.

2 **Learning at my own pace**
   I was hassled in school to do things quickly and I can't. I'm like the tortoise, in the story of the Hare and the Tortoise, which we acted out at COGS. I get there in the end.

3 **Learning that gives me choices**
   In school a lot of what we did was not for me – it wasn't what I needed to sort my life at that moment. I wanted help with understanding things and getting over what I thought clearly but only my parents saw this. Schools seem only interested in what they think we need to be taught and in the grades we get for our work.

Eddy's comments are coloured by unhappy feelings about school. As in all social experiences, some will thrive while others die. What's meat for one is poison for another. There is no social experience that will suit all participants and school is no exception to this general rule.

TASK: Make a list of what is important for your learning. Your issues may be different to Eddy's. Try out the task with some students to get a feel of a general point of view.

◆ Learning as a social experience

Does it shock you to learn that 73 per cent of children enter school with insufficient language and communication skills to cope with this social learning experience?

A study in Sheffield provides this evidence (Lees and co-workers, 2001), and is supported by the Carnegie research (Boyer, 1992) which uncovered a similar pattern in the USA. The statistics are alarming: the overwhelming majority of teachers (7,000) cited lack of proficiency in language as being the area in which students were most deficient; 98 per cent of children on school entry were regarded as having communication problems, and 51 per cent of these were serious. My own pilot research confirms this tendency and findings suggest that children do not make up their deficits without specific help.

The notion of the child as a problem solver, designer and builder of his own knowledge is entirely compatible with the views of eminent educationalists such as Piaget (1967). Bruner (1966) viewed instruction as helping to find manageable problems. Accepting the child's natural problem-solving and self-instructional abilities does not imply that their interactions and encounters are not crucial to what and how they learn. Robinson (1981) argued that intellectual and language development are progressed by specific social experiences. Students can be helped to increase thinking and understanding by becoming more explicitly aware of the processes through which they communicate and learn. Eddy bears this out in his review of what helps him to cope with learning activities. His need to sort out his communication was fundamental to his ability to cope with school.

Studies of adolescents, however, portray a grim picture of children's natural thinking and communicative abilities. They also suggest that the right kind of educational experience plays a vital role in determining to what extent students are able to gain knowledge and expertise and use language to explain, instruct and self-regulate. In a large study of adolescents' communication skills, Brown and co-workers (1984) worked with 500 young people between 14 and 17 years of age in Scotland who were considered unlikely to leave school with formal academic achievements. Students were observed talking informally in pairs and seen to be chatty and amusing, presenting as confident and competent communicators. Minor increases in communication demands, however, produced marked impairments in performance. When asked to talk on a tape recorder these students' speech was much less fluent and articulate than in the face-to-face situation. The absence of live partners, to supply verbal and non-verbal support, had a major impact on the quality of communication. Asking the students to give detailed instructions and explanations to others produced a further deterioration in performances.

◆ Different communication styles inside and outside class

Underpinning the research in Scotland is an important distinction between informal and formal speaking. Informal speech is chat that might be about anything and go anywhere. It is typically mundane and requires little analytic ability. Formal speech is directed towards a specific goal, as in giving a set of instructions or retelling an experience. It requires an ability to structure events and provide a coherent discourse. Both informal and formal communication is bound by implicit conventions. In chat, we refrain from probing too far and respect people's beliefs and behaviour, although the boundaries will depend on the intimacy of the relationships between participants. In formal talk, there is less chance for interaction, so we pitch information at a level that we judge the audience can cope with comfortably, and organize it so that it is readily understood.

Differences in the underlying purposes of talk in and outside class are reflected in the nature of the relationship between those involved and their use of language in a particular situation. For example, a study by Pate and Bremer (1967) found that 69 per cent of questions to students in class were to check knowledge, whereas outside class students experience questions performing a wider variety of functions. Fourteen years later, Stodolsky and co-workers (1981) reported a similar pattern, with only 20 per cent of classroom questions being devoted to thinking beyond recall. Often, teacher questions violate established conventions; teachers expect answers to questions such as 'Jack, why are you sniffing?' even though they flout normal ideas of what is polite. Getting answers right is a principal concern of teachers, with students expected to justify what they say. Children are often confused by this switch in conventions and are incapable of giving answers because to do so involves the construction of comprehensible narratives, which they are not skilled at producing.

To remedy this lack of narrative ability, Brown and co-workers designed tasks to help foster student skills in giving information and instruction, coaching both listener and speaker roles. The process ended with a specific assessment to give value to the activities in the students' eyes. The result was a massive increase in personal and academic performance, with the students achieving well in their final leaving certificates against original predictions. Once students were able to process and express information clearly and logically, learning became a rewarding experience. The research highlights the problems of students understanding teachers and coming to grips with new forms of communicating. Inability to process large amounts of information, as well as to organize, regulate and express what is known in a coherent way, would appear to be a major handicap to any satisfactory school progress.

So what are the implications of such evidence? Teachers must be aware of their students' diverse skills in coping with classroom communication and learning. With figures suggesting that around three-quarters of our children enter school with language and communication well below that needed to process learning, we have much to concern ourselves about. Those with English as a second language require this attention as a priority for dealing with information in a less familiar format.

TASK: Do you know whether your students understand what you teach them? How can you test for this? Specific questions on what you have said are not the way to check comprehension. Get students, in pairs, to summarize the information you have just given, in just one minute. Is it possible to record some samples?

◆ Do schools help children learn?

In the introduction to this chapter, a case study was presented suggesting that at least one school-age student (Eddy) has been unable to cope with today's sophisticated school learning system. His schools could not account for his learning differences and he felt like a square peg in a round hole. Education is an experience that is founded in a body of knowledge not only of how children learn, but also what they should be taught and how they should be organized for this. Eddy mentions this as a problem for him in his educational review (page 106).

In various sections of this book, we have discussed how children learn, and reflected on how they pick up knowledge and understanding in different ways and at different rates. In a way, the idea of a genuinely child-centred culture is nonsense, as young children must learn about the whole community they are born into and prepare for their place in it. Trends in society bring child and adult together but also force them apart. Longer periods of education are prolonging children's dependent status; even postgraduate students may find themselves still living with their parents, these days!

Nowadays, the intellectual gap between an educated adult and a growing child is so large that only sophisticated learning systems can bridge it. The spread of higher education and increasing technical complexity of so much adult work has exaggerated the differences between child and adult worlds. This has enormous implications for education, which must address the needs of a society with complex, technical activities. The workplace has witnessed a massive shift away from heavy industry towards the 'people services' requiring levels of personal skill not previously considered necessary to acquire in a formal, educated way. Presently, there appears to be a mismatch between skills required in the world of work and those that schools are required to deliver (Mason, 1996).

In its broader sense, education is about acquiring and using knowledge, developing our mental abilities to understand, as well as gaining personal skills of communication, co-operation and collaboration. The latter abilities are vital in making an inclusive school philosophy work, as students must be able to participate with others to be involved equally in what goes on in school. There is also an expectation that schools can cure social ills and compensate for poverty, abuse and any other personal difficulties that a child might bring into school. Clearly this is nonsense when teachers have so much curriculum content with which to concern themselves.

Since the 1981 Education Act, students have been able to acquire a legal statement entitling them to extra support in school if their learning difficulties are long term and severe. Teaching assistants have fulfilled this role, and are playing an increasingly important part in helping the education system to work for a diverse population of students. However, research (Sage and Sommefeldt, 2004) shows that only around 1 per cent of staff in schools have accredited training in learning support. Extra opportunities for children are lost if they are not expertly applied with a proper knowledge and understanding of learning differences and difficulties.

◆ Functions of education

Academic knowledge, understanding and skills

The traditional skills of reading, writing and arithmetic are essential to survive a modern world. As we seek to raise standards there are increasing numbers of children who require help to achieve the expected attainment targets at each of the Key Stages. Support staff play a major role here. At the root of most basic skill difficulties is an inability to cope well with language and communication, so that students need help to access learning with specific intervention or counselling. Cooper (2001) has reviewed schemes and recommends the Communication Opportunity Group Scheme (COGS) (Sage, 2000a), circle time (Mosley, 1996) and nurture groups (Boxall, 1996), as successful ways of helping children to develop confidence and basic abilities to cope with learning.

The Communication Opportunity Group Scheme concentrates on developing thinking and communication in both spoken and written tasks, whereas circle time and nurture groups are built on the idea of encouraging talk to facilitate self-esteem. The development of transferable, key/core abilities is essential if students are to become part of an adaptable, flexible workforce of the skills economy, along with ICT. Thus, communication as well as literacy and numeracy have been promoted up the agenda, particularly within post-16 learning. This will increasingly become a speciality for teaching assistants in schools, as studies discussed earlier point to the fact that children do not have sufficient grip of school communication styles to cope successfully with their learning.

Socialization, social order and self-control

Socialization is a process of induction into society's culture, norms and values. This ensures a level of social cohesion necessary for society to continue. School, along with the family, has a crucial role here. In order to live a safe and ordered life, we must be aware of the expected ways to behave. These may be viewed as norms of behaviour, or manners. Think about how we conduct ourselves in an orderly manner for much of our lives without thinking about it. We say 'please' and 'thank you' in appropriate circumstances, learn to queue for school meals and file into class from the playground. In public places, such as school corridors, we walk sensibly without bumping into others and touching people. We also maintain appropriate distance and eye contact when talking with others.

These social communication norms are learned and educators are crucial in this process. Much of what they do is incidental to academic tasks – reminding children not to talk while the teacher does, to take turns and not to push and shove while waiting for something. All through the school day, adults are pointing children in the direction of good social communication, control and order. Teaching assistants, who focus on the child to complement teachers' concentration on the curriculum, have a major responsibility for facilitating a child's social learning.

Preparation for work

In small, self-sufficient societies, children learn survival from surrounding adults, who are multi-skilled and can satisfy most needs. In these contexts, the adult is a *mentor* rather than someone who stands in front of a group and transmits knowledge. As forms of employment have diversified and become specialized, specific education and training is needed in schools, colleges and universities. The general qualities required for employment, such as those expressed in the transferable skills, can be developed at all levels of education. Job-specific training is often based in the workplace, but is more and more likely to involve further and higher education in continuing professional development programmes. Preparing students for work is increasingly seen as an important role for schools. This is an ideal specialization area for support staff, involving personal coaching – the skill developed from their work with individual children.

Overlap and interaction of functions

These functions of education may appear to overlap. Preparation for work involves personal skills such as communication, planning, problem solving and collaboration, as well as developing the mind and acquiring relevant knowledge. Socialization and internalized social control are also a part of this. Different functions may be to the fore at various stages of a student's education. Whereas it is appropriate to target the development of the mind, expression of thinking and individual freedom to explore and experiment, it is also important to stress discipline and self-control to fit into school and also society.

Although all functions are appropriate, together they may cause tensions. For example, developing thinking and communication encourages a questioning attitude, but the need to maintain social order involves obedience and correct behaviour. The latter could be viewed as developing *accepting* rather than *questioning* individuals. Educators encourage students to question issues in topics which are studied. Work in primary schools is largely investigative and with the emphasis on science and technology children are constantly required to ask questions to do with electricity, friction, different materials, life cycles of plants and animals and so on. In other areas of school life, however – such as lesson choice, homework, discipline, uniform, tests, examinations and so on – there is no room for questioning and children have to buckle down and conform. Obedience is a virtue, listed alongside independence and initiative, and employers also require it in large measure. A balance has to be struck, therefore, between *self-development* and *self-control* and the educator's function is to support and encourage students in this process. This needs clear understanding about human nature, the working of schools and the purposes of activities, which this book has tried to present.

The emphasis placed on the varied functions of education may be different according to the student's potential and performance level. Some students may be pushed academically because they are good at mental tasks; others will be encouraged in sport or practical skills because this is where they shine. Davis and Moore (1967) saw this sifting of talent and allocating of individuals to appropriate roles in society as an important function of a formal education system.

Some argue, however, that too much time is spent theorizing about education, taking time away from the real issues. This assumes agreement of what learning is and how it should be conducted. Chris Woodhead (Ofsted, 2000), then Chief Inspector of Schools, wrote in his annual report:

> We know what constitutes good teaching and we know what needs to be done to tackle weaknesses: we must strengthen subject knowledge, raise expectations, and hone the pedagogic skills upon which the craft of the classroom depends ... Why, then, is so much time and energy wasted in research that complicates what ought to be straightforward?

This apparent rejection of alternatives could be viewed as an attempt to prevent debate and silence dissent. Research has been important, not only in understanding the child and how she learns best, but also in pointing out the strengths and weaknesses of policies and practices. Because of its ideological base, the organization of learning will always be an important aspect of politics (Carr and Hartnett, 1996). It is a central and increasingly important aspect of a complex, technological society that needs sophisticated knowledge and skills to compete in the global economy. Education helps shape the future, not only in developing individuals, but also by promoting ideas. As active participants in society, we have our own views on learning and how it should be structured. The interaction of competing interests renders it a stimulating and fascinating study.

TASK: What do you think are the most important things in which to educate students? What is the basis for your views? Choose a learning experience from your own education. What impact did it have on you? How does it relate to your views on educating children? Identifying these issues is important, as they influence how you organize learning.

◆ The national curriculum for England

Education in England has evolved from an elitist to an inclusive system with a national curriculum that all state schools must follow. Appendix 5 (page 173) provides a historical context. The present system is far from satisfactory for all children and there have been major criticisms.

Although many educationalists agree with the principles of the national curriculum, they deplore its installation and development (Lawton, 1999). Complaints relate to an absence of clear educational purpose, a disregard for learning development, and a failure to consult with teachers and others on content and its implementation. Cajkler and Hislam (2002), for example, provide evidence to show how grammar has been misconceived and misapplied in the national curriculum. Cajkler (1999, 2002) demonstrates the muddles and confusions emanating from government literature and says:

> ... there are now so many documents that it is not easy to find time to analyse, piece together and use them in an informed way.

The introduction of standard age-related tests means that children are ranked and ordered as never before and their value to the school and to potential workplaces depends on these results. The fact that children have varying abilities, interests and backgrounds logically supposes that they need different learning experiences. Diversity has to be preserved and valued for a successful society. What seems to be at fault is the notion that academic education is best for all. The push to send 50 per cent of our children into universities denies the importance of the practical intelligences.

We need *thinkers*, but also more *doers*, to keep the world turning and must cultivate attitudes that value practical careers as equally desirable as academic ones. Recently, I attended hospital in the middle of the night with a very sick mother, who was in Accident and Emergency for five hours while being assessed. It was the cleaner who chatted, made tea and gave support. His role in hospital services was vital, and yet medical professionals conveyed their assumed superiority in the way they dealt with him. As long as we put academic knowledge on a pedestal, other forms of knowledge, such as knowing how to care for someone, will never be seen as equitable.

There is tension in our modern educational arrangements. We aim to include a diverse range of students but require them all to learn in a similar way and reach standard norms at the same time. What sense is this? Our knowledge of brain sciences defies a single goal and a single approach that encompasses all human needs.

TASK: Visit the DfES website (www.dfes.gov.uk) and look up publications on educational developments. Read through some to identify key areas of education policy and practice. How do these ideas match your own thinking on the subject?

◆ Putting ideas into practice

The impact of different ideas and beliefs is seen in what and how we teach children. However, knowledge can be structured and presented in different ways and at different stages. Traditional subjects may be seen as contextually important and information presented in themes to reflect current affairs. For example, the theme 'How people live' can include all subject areas and be organized for any age or ability group, embracing facts as well as providing opportunities for key skill development.

113

Learning and teaching can take many forms, depending on the purpose of the curriculum and the beliefs and skills of educators. The emphasis may be on practical applications, experimentation, direct teaching or open learning, where the child has materials to work through alone in their own way. A mixture of methods is often applied, but we all have our favourite approaches, which reflect our own preferences. Support staff often work across classes and observe that students have very different experiences according to a teacher's personal learning and communication style. One teacher may emphasize an interactive, oral approach whereas another will transmit information 'one-way', and target writing and rote learning. Support staff must understand why these variations occur and be flexible enough to fit in with the particular organizing genres of the classes in which they work, as well as the processing and representational styles of both students and teachers.

How do educators organize learning?

There are now many different professionals working in schools, and their roles have begun to show some differentiation, as they take responsibility for various areas of the educational process. The teaching assistant, learning mentor and student counsellor are more concerned with the details of children, while the teacher targets the subjects of the curriculum, their implementation and assessment. Roles should be considered as complementary and equal in importance but with a different emphasis in education and training. Teachers develop subject knowledge and ways to transmit this, whereas other educators acquire therapeutic skills that help children learn.

Support staff usually work with individuals or small groups and understanding the dynamics is essential for successful learning. Individuals in a small group communicate face-to-face but the participants exercise a special influence on everybody's behaviour. Many studies (for example, Gill and Adams, 1989) have looked at what makes groups work. There has to be a goal, and once everyone understands this, there is a process of 'storming, norming and performing'. 'Storming' is the settling in period when participants reveal their differences and personalities; some may be overbearing and even disruptive. 'Norming' is the establishing of rules and the ways in which the group of individuals will operate and behave. 'Performing' happens when the structure of operations is decided and work can start.

Each time a group convenes this process occurs, but the two initial phases are accelerated in an established arrangement. All processes still need acknowledging, however, in warm-up activities to get children relating to one another and remind them of the rules of operation. Studies have shown that groups without a leader have very unequal participation, where the active ones make the decisions and the passive ones agree. If you leave children to work on their own you need to discuss their roles and observe:

- ◆ behaviour that helps complete the task
- ◆ behaviour that strengthens the group and values contributions
- ◆ behaviour that disrupts the group's work.

Of interest to educators is the difference between a led group (wheel, with the leader at the 'hub') and a non-led one (open circle). The following table clarifies differences between led and non-led groups.

	Led group (wheel)	Non-led group (circle)
Direction	Control centred on one person, resulting in a tendency to one-to-one communication.	No one in control and two-way communication occurs because more channels are available.
Speed	Group reaches decisions quickly.	Group takes longer to reach decisions because there is more participation.
Accuracy	More likely to be inaccurate because there is less feedback. There is less danger of irrelevant issues interfering with the task.	More contributions giving extensive information and chance to correct errors. There is scope for digressions and irrelevancies.
Morale	Less involvement on the part of most members leads to lower morale.	More participation by everyone brings higher group morale.

The overall conclusions of research suggest that:

◆ the one who handles the most information has the most status in the group

◆ people like to set up routines and procedures, and keep to them

◆ people enjoy working in groups where they have most participation.

Groups play a vital role in classroom learning and need identity and purpose. An effective group allows members to discover who they are and what they want to achieve. It also provides support for participants' development, encouraging communication, co-operation and collaboration to reach the group goal. It is vital to observe the groups in which children work best and check that all students have a chance to participate. Research has looked at this aspect and one aim of the Communication Opportunity Group Scheme is to teach children group skills so that they can learn effectively (Sage, 2000a and 2000b). Some children do not have the communication skills to cope with a group, however, and pair situations are the best setting in which to develop these, as long as the partnership remains equal and the less able child is not dominated. Support staff often work with children in a pair but must ensure that they do not do all the talking and that they allow the students to have control. It is easy to have the upper hand with children who lack communication skills and talk *for* them and *at* them rather than *with* them.

◆ Developing interactive teaching and learning: the Critical Skills Programme

Prescriptive education, such as that associated with the national curriculum for England, leads to transmission teaching, where the adult delivers information with minimal opportunities for interaction with students, other than streams of questioning to check their knowledge. This leads to passive learners who know facts but do not fully understand them because they have not been challenged to work in collaborative ways that would enhance their appreciation. If we are to develop the personal skills of students that will help them be successful learners, we have to find ways to balance the 'learning by listening' with a 'learning by talking' approach.

Not all teachers, however, embrace this interactive approach easily. Sage and Cwenar (2003), in a project looking at learning and teaching, found that 40 per cent of educators were uncomfortable with interactive learning, which is an important issue to consider if trying to establish this method in schools. The Critical Skills Programme is a way to help teachers train in such a strategy.

In 2000, the Critical Skills Programme (CSP) (Mobilia and co-workers, 2001) was introduced into Britain through Network Educational Press. The aim was to enhance learning and improve behaviour in the classroom by engaging students in learning experiences, some including collaborative challenges, based on an interactive approach. CSP started in New Hampshire, USA, in 1982. It has since spread to neighbouring states and is designed to help students develop:

- **critical skills** (known in Britain as key or transferable skills) – problem solving, decision making, critical thinking, communication, organization, management, leadership
- **fundamental dispositions** – life-long learning, self-direction, internal model of quality, integrity and ethical character, collaboration, curiosity and wonder, community membership.

UK training is provided by Network Educational Press and is available in Level 1 and 2 workshops, which can lead to an accredited Post-Graduate Diploma in Higher Education by the University of Leicester. The diploma may be continued into a Masters programme through distance or open learning. At Level 1 teachers:

- experience CSP activities as students
- learn how to create a collaborative classroom community
- learn how to design problem-solving challenges, which form the focus of the class model.

The core activities of CSP are *challenges*, which are complex, open-ended problems designed to cover mainstream curriculum content at all levels, from nursery children through to adult learners. They aim to promote:

- deeper understanding and greater retention of subject knowledge
- critical skills and fundamental dispositions (see above)
- regular reflection and review of personal learning goals
- purposeful and effective use of information technology.

After further classroom experience, teachers can then develop their understanding of the model at Level 2 and progress through Level 3 to become Co-ordinators.

The programme has wide support from British teachers, which proves the need for this approach. There is much anecdotal evidence of its success, and on-going scientific studies based at Lancaster University and the University of the West of England are collecting data that, provisionally, indicates substantial improvement of results in participating schools. The programme puts together an exciting collection of activities, which are based on the practical knowledge of very experienced and talented teachers. Some caution is required, though, regarding its use with students, who may have specific problems in the higher order thinking required by the CSP challenges. There is much research pointing out the fact that children do not generalize what they have learned, if this does not sit within recognized developmental frameworks that make such links possible (summarized by Wilde, 2004).

What is the philosophical base for Critical Skills?

The strategy draws on reconstructionist ideas that focus on a vital issue: *how should we educate our citizens for the twenty-first century?* Key philosophers have suggested that the numbing and neutering uniformities of industrial modernization have led to apathy and conformity among people. A fear of difference causes tension in our diverse multicultural societies. The question is, *how can we live and work positively and creatively with each other?*

To counteract the present system of domination operating in society (Wink, 1992), we need new ways of interacting. In order to cope with the world we must *filter* vast quantities of information, *question* situations and *receive feedback* on our performances – the abilities identified by old theologians as Diakrisis (discerning, distinguishing, judging), without which people would become 'dupe to the devil' and 'a mouthpiece of their mentors' (Merry, 2000). The skill to read situations, make appropriate judgements and respond effectively only develops through active dialogue with others, exposing us to a range of ideas and solutions; the Critical Skills Programme provides a structure for doing this. Only when we have these skills will we be able to achieve openness, cope with challenge and change, and accept difference.

Traditions in teaching

We operate, however, within a powerful set of educational traditions, which illustrate how values, cultural contexts, practical experiences, research findings and intellectual movements have combined and influenced our thinking about living and learning. The three major ideologies are summarized below in order to help us understand our positions.

- ◆ **Classical humanism** seeks to maintain established standards of cultural excellence through student selection methods. Subject disciplines, the examination system and selective education are rooted in this tradition. Personal and academic abilities are valued.

- ◆ **Progressivism** focuses on the development of individual potential and fulfilment. These ideas are behind comprehensive education and arguments against selection. A focus on catering for individual need encourages flexible learning and discourages standard comparisons between students.

- ◆ **Reconstructionism** emphasizes learning as an active, interpersonal process, guided but not dominated by educators. Education is seen as playing a major role in social renewal. There is an emphasis on communal learning, participation and action.

Critical Skill Programmes are grounded in reconstructionist ideas, promoted originally by Plato, and in the twentieth century by the American, John Dewey (1975). Dewey's aspiration was to make a new kind of citizen, *better* and more effective that the average, present one. Education is, thus, seen as an agent for social renewal. Whereas classical humanism and progressivism are a familiar part of the British educational scene, reconstructionism has never been as popular as in the United States or the developing countries.

The relative disinterest in reconstructionism among most industrial societies, and its rapid rise in the developing nations, suggests a relationship between educational theory and the social, political context from which it develops. Traditional, stable societies are generally satisfied with institutions and their policies and so do not promote doctrines to revise the social order. It is periods of crisis or social upheaval that find a ready audience for reconstructionist views.

In the writings of Illich (1971, 1981), Freire (1972), Foucault (1984), and more recently Eco (2001), Wink (1992), Handy (1994), Barber (1995) and Hillman (1995), social and educational theory has acquired a strong, radical and political tone, expressing a deep dissatisfaction with existing tendencies and arrangements in society. Examples are also seen in documents from the United Nations Educational, Scientific and Cultural Organization (UNESCO) and the Organisation for Economic Co-operation and Development (OECD). These stress the impetus towards basic cultural change, precipitated by the modernizing processes of technology, industrialization and democracy. Education is seen to be the key process in reducing social conflict and developing new, more successful patterns for living and learning.

The goals of reconstructing social order are different for Plato and the modernists. For Plato, the objective was cultural stability, dependent on the discovery and preservation of truth, which was a task for the ruling classes. Truth, according to Plato, is beyond the reach and interest of the masses, for which entertainment is more appropriate. Entertainment was part of the process of conditioning the masses into acceptance of whatever the rulers determined. Aldous Huxley, a modern political satirist, has developed this view in *Brave New World*, presenting frightening images of mass conditioning and authoritarian rule. The elitists rule out the common man's perfectibility as being against his *nature*.

Today's views of reconstructionist ideas

Modern reconstructionists, influenced by nineteenth-century democratic theory and the Age of Enlightenment, envisaged spiritual and intellectual advance and social and economic improvements for the whole of society. The pursuit of the perfect human requires the removal of a barrier to human improvement, the doctrine of original sin – a belief playing a large part in our traditional approaches to punishment in schools.

The ideas of modern reconstructionists have been influenced by the Enlightenment view of man's rationality and the cultivation of this as a primary goal of education. Today, we are not so naively confident as the Enlightenment thinkers about the inevitability of social and cultural progress, given the sustained application of science to human affairs. The solution to one problem generally brings many more difficulties in its wake (for example, in medicine, the treatment of heart failure using 'spare part surgery' brings new problems such as rejection of the transplanted tissues, side effects of drugs and survival in vegetative states).

Steady improvement is encouraged, however, achieved through long-term, large-scale attempts to plan and organize individual and social experience according to agreed goals and procedures. Such plans need proper structures for participation, a general consensus and the pursuit of common goals for everybody. The Tanzanian social project, led by President Nyerere, is an example of how these principles worked successfully in the 1970s but have now lost momentum. From an educational point of view, what is important is the deliberate cultivation of rationality, problem-solving strategies, adaptability, flexibility and a general ability to communicate and face up to the practical realities of life. Everything else is seen as secondary to this personal development.

An open thought system

Reconstructionism, therefore, is an open thought system capable of absorbing many influences and precipitating new possibilities for action. It is interested in the interaction of ideas and changing social and cultural environments. There have been many uses of *environment*, not just as a context in which change occurs, but also as a contrast with influences of *heredity* in shaping human behaviour. Reconstructionists describe humans as having potential for growth with a plastic, malleable nature, and consider social institutions and traditions in terms such as modifiability, flexibility and fluidity. This contrasts markedly with the classical humanist interest in putting people into rigid, unchangeable categories. Today, the education system in England slots everyone into one inclusive category, with a 'one size fits all' approach to learning. Issues such as common-core curricula, mixed-ability grouping and different forms of student assessment reflect people's views of human nature and their commitments to various philosophies.

Reconstructionists are conscious of the vulnerability of human beings to commercial and political manipulation. Some have advocated propaganda as a counter to persuasion and manipulation, although Dewey felt this was defeating for a theory based on reflective enquiry and cultural renewal through education.

Summary of main ideas underlying Critical Skills

To summarize this context for the Critical Skill Programme, it would appear that reconstructionism identifies tasks faced by society in periods of rapid, large-scale cultural change and specifies the skills needed by people involved. These are not only academic skills but, most importantly, personal abilities that allow people to communicate and learn successfully in their social contexts. Although some would justify attempts by educators to transmit only established knowledge, this loses credibility when the world which gave rise to knowledge disciplines is changing at an increasingly rapid rate and requiring more personal skills of everyone. Focusing on the characteristics, trends and problems of contemporary culture, as distinct from the past, is vital. Today's world needs, above all, people who are confident communicators, who can control their experiences and manage their lives successfully. The evidence presented in this text suggests that we cannot assume children acquire such skills naturally, and educators must take this into account to fit students for living and working. Disregarding present circumstances could destroy or change the whole nature of our society. New cultural selections and definitions of tasks are required; new socially unifying values are advocated; new modes of teaching are suggested to cope with the pace and scope of change and give students the personal and knowledge skills to cope. The Critical Skill Programme has developed within this philosophy.

Criticisms of these views

Critics (for example, Bantock, 1968) of these new directionist views have denounced them as too abstract and Utopian. The conviction that people can choose the life, society and culture they want appears unrealistic and against the forces of the universe. Moreover, the teacher plays a creative and crucial role. His job is not merely to spread ideas but to appraise the attributes of modern culture and work for its renewal. It demands much more than the transmission of knowledge. This is both a challenge and a weakness. Do teachers have the skills, desire, remit and resources to carry out such a role? Merry (2000) says not and suggests that the organization called Engage! Interact would play a part in helping teachers prepare for this new role. The Critical Skills Programme Co-ordinators aim to play a similar function, helping educators to move from transmission to interactive teaching modes – to develop both thinking and reflective students who are collectively better able to solve the problems of the modern world, and thinking and reflective educators who form part of the collaborative learning community established in their classrooms.

Issues regarding implementation of new approaches

Without large-scale alterations in government philosophy and training schemes, there is little likelihood of new modes of learning and teaching being widely adopted – though there are positive indications of increasing interest in interactive approaches. The national curriculum for England is based on the goal of equal opportunity and the same standards for all. In a devastating attack on the way the Government's inclusion policy is being implemented, parents of the newly formed Special School Protection League (www.gsspl.org.uk) are campaigning for *extra* rather than *equal* opportunities in education. Inclusion of their children in mainstream schools has been a failure, and parents argue that they would be better prepared for participation in the outside world in small classes where teachers have specific expertise to target key skill development before that of subject knowledge. Human Scale Education, an educational charity, was set up to promote such values – a holistic approach to learning, a democratic structure and a partnership with parents in helping children to achieve personal skills first and academic abilities thereafter.

The curriculum is thus a key issue. In contrast to classical humanism and progressivism, reconstructionism requires subject matter to be treated explicitly in terms of contemporary issues. Science is given a prominent place because it reflects, incorporates and expresses modern experience, with concepts and methods to organize and direct change. The social sciences provide knowledge of humankind's potential for action (defined in key skills), while the physical sciences show our capacity to make sense of and use the world's resources. Also, the reconstructionist method of rational, reflective enquiry is based on the scientific model of suggestion, problem, hypothesis, reasoning and testing. This process is followed in the Critical Skill Programme challenges. Reflective experiences change and modify situations, beliefs and knowledge. In this model, the individual learns to take responsibility and is no longer a passive recipient of messages and commands but an agent of development and renewal.

Abandoning completely traditional disciplines, their approaches and assessment, would rob us of the possibility of understanding our present position and attaining a sound, basic knowledge of society and its evolution. For example, the study of Latin delivers major benefits for the understanding of English language and literature, foreign languages and history. For getting across strong, simple ideas about word function, Latin is unmatched. It also helps in the study of medicine and law, as many anatomical and judicial terms are Latin words. Since the theory involves nurturing individuals and preparing them for an active role in social change, there is always a danger that enthusiasm could lead to dubious methods. Aldous Huxley's Brave New World is an extreme, fictional example. In that novel, the aim was to reconstruct society to provide the maximum pleasure for the maximum number of people. Genetic engineering was used and people indoctrinated into accepting their place in society, which offered most satisfaction for them. As satirized by Huxley, social engineering has the distinctly scary goal of predicting and controlling the future!

Problems with theories of change

The reconstructionist ideology emphasizes the participatory role of all citizens. There might be tension between the desire to bring about predictable change and the view that education should necessarily enable the student to make judgements. It seems impossible to know in advance what direction will be taken by a population educated to exercise their own judgements. Also, the notion of people being able to participate equally seems fraught with difficulty, as the Special School Protection League has vociferously pointed out (page 120).

There is a danger, therefore, that educational methods – though seen as promoting freedom and equality – could be tainted by the specific beliefs of educators. There is an old joke that patients treated by Freud had Freudian dreams, while those by Jung had Jungian dreams. Nyerere, for example, promoted particular social changes through education in Tanzania (page 118) and there is controversy as to whether these have been entirely good for the country.

In the context of this debate, it is important to note that it is just as possible to indoctrinate people with liberal views as fascist ones, and may be just as common. The particular danger is the assumption that individuals can in some sense make free choices about how they might learn and conduct their lives, and choose to adopt some values and not others. Determinists would challenge this and claim that individuals were being conditioned to accept certain views in any event.

Arguments can get very abstract. A recent newspaper article, 'Don't tell us what to think', berates politicians for refusing open and honest discussion of society's problems. This clearly reinforces a view of domination and the need for liberation. In schools, we pour knowledge into students at an ever-increasing rate, giving them no time to think and communicate their views. We are grateful for any attempt to help teachers and their students reflect on the salient issues in life in a little more depth. The Critical Skills Programme should be promoted, as we owe the next generation a voice in creating their world. Nevertheless, we need to take on board that the reflective enquiry involved in the challenges demands a level of thinking and communication that a significant number of students could not achieve without a specific programme that aims to facilitate thinking and expressive abilities. The Communication Opportunity Group Scheme offers a complementary approach in preparing students to acquire such skills.

That such skills are needed, but often ignored, is evident in this extract from a report about a student called Jamie (not his real name) who was excluded from a senior school:

Jamie has no obvious problems in the area of speech and language other than his poor reasoning skills. His comprehension is satisfactory and he communicates in an articulate fashion. He is able to talk clearly about his antisocial behaviour and presents as a student within the top ability range of the MLD cohort.

The statement is ambiguous, suggesting good communication but poor reasoning. He is competent at informal talk but is like the students in the Scottish study (Brown and co-workers, 1984) whose performance deteriorated greatly in formal speaking. A narrative thinking and discourse problem is evident but there is no mention of this in the report and no strategy for support. Jamie is representative of many students who need clearer identification of their performance differences and difficulties.

◆ Review

Education is an extremely complex business in today's society. The idea of globalization, for instance, impacts on how we think about the relations between culture, identity, institutions and practices. Post-colonial migrations have brought us a rich multicultural society, where communities with different value systems, forms of identity and social practices may live side by side with one another, mingle, mix and interact. Schools play a vital role in providing opportunities, experiences and structures for a range of cultural identities and personal differences to find positive expression. The present world no longer has fixed bearings and traditional explanations no longer apply, because cultural intermingling is the order of the day.

In this shifting, uncertain and unstable world of difference, education has to operate and manage knowledge, culture, conduct and values. Failure to engage positively with the diversity that children bring into school results in damaging inequalities. Eddy, our case study (page 105), demonstrates how the dominant quest for standards has thrown student needs off the learning agenda. Although many problems remain in implementing an inclusive education policy for students like Eddy, progress has been made. New breeds of educators are important forces in making this work, offering a fresh perspective in school practice, and providing therapeutic experiences for the increasing number of children who need extra learning support. For example, teaching assistants are emerging professionals, offering degree-level qualifications and real knowledge and expertise of today's school system. In senior schools, learning mentors, counsellors and curriculum managers are found, providing fresh skills to enhance the educational process.

Today, we demand a great deal of our educators, who are right to say that much of what they struggle against is imported from outside school. They cannot be expected to fight society's battles alone. There is a price to pay, however, for an education system dominated by credentials; those who do not achieve them are deemed, and deem themselves, as failures. Over the last ten years the number of children identified as having special needs has increased by 40 per cent and these pose a grave risk to the stability of society if they cannot achieve their potential. Part of the price for our present system is the vast amount of educator's time devoted to 'pastoral care', which is too often a synonym for containing poor communication and bad behaviour from students who are unable to cope with the system.

But strategies do work, and this text has mentioned particularly the Communication Opportunity Group Scheme and the Critical Skills Programme that aim to balance academic with personal abilities in support of learning. The importance of personal skills, particularly communication, from which all others spring, has been a consistent theme over the last

30 years (Brigman and co-workers, 1999), but one that has not been implemented. Maybe educators feel that personal skills should not be their primary concern when they are forced to concentrate on academic performance for league tables. Also, personal skill approaches demand interactive teaching, which has not been strongly promoted so that teachers lack the training to implement them effectively.

These abilities, however, are the key to academic success for the diverse cultures that come together in schools. Programmes focusing on personal performance promote the ability to negotiate the different backgrounds and norms of children, helping them acquire the skills needed for achievement, while retaining, valuing and applying their specific styles and ways of behaving. Teele (2000) cites research suggesting that schools valuing personal development, as well as academic skills, score at least 20 per cent above average grades and have few behaviour problems. Gardner (1993) suggests that students just go through the motions of education and are unable to apply knowledge and skills to new situations. They need to become active learners through group dialogue, rather than passive listeners in the process of learning. Perhaps we have some of the answers for dealing with a world of difference. All we have to do now is close our eyes, jump and see where it lands us – not in the soup, but the sea of success!

Main Points

- ◆ Education has evolved from an elitist to an inclusive system, aiming to provide equal opportunities but not necessarily extra opportunities for those who need them.
- ◆ Anxieties have been expressed regarding the national curriculum for England, as it ranks children in a public way to a greater extent than ever before, affecting children's life chances.
- ◆ Education has a remit to develop not only academic but social and life skills, to prepare children for jobs and participation in communities, but emphasis on academic skills for league tables pushes other considerations aside.
- ◆ Our multicultural society ensures that children not only have diverse abilities and interests but very different backgrounds and values, which education has to merge and manage.
- ◆ The Communication Opportunity Group Scheme and Critical Skills Programme have been tailored to develop children's thinking and communicating ability, offering a chance of personal and academic success that may not be possible otherwise.
- ◆ Interactive styles of teaching move away from traditional approaches but are not actively promoted by policy and practice makers.
- ◆ Support staff play a major role in developing inclusive schools and coping with diversity, by providing therapeutic support for a large range of needs. The curriculum could be balanced by training them to deliver key skills for students, so strengthening their learning base.

Approaches to developing communication and learning

◆ The Communication Opportunity Group Scheme

The Communication Opportunity Group Scheme (Sage, 2000) developed from a Medical Research Council project in the 1980s and 1990s to discover why some children failed in school. The conclusion was that these children's narrative structure competence (giving directions, explanations, accounts, reports) was underdeveloped, preventing them from expressing their thoughts coherently and negotiating their lives successfully. Understanding words and individual sentences was not a problem but connecting up ideas from large chunks of talk or text was much more difficult.

The COGS is based on the idea of social involvement as the springboard for thinking. True communication is a discursive dialogue – an exchange where meaning is actively pursued. Ideas are developed in relation to their *clarity*, appropriate *content* for the occasion, knowledge of the *conventions* that express information and awareness of the *conduct* that transmits impressions to others, influencing the communication exchange through feedback. There are fourteen levels, matching primary, secondary and tertiary educational requirements, based on five learning principles:

1. co-operation in a group
2. empathy for others
3. active learning
4. learner-centred activities chosen by participants
5. message-oriented communication (verbal and non-verbal language used as communication, including not only words but gestures, movements, facial expressions, tone of voice and props – pictures or objects that might form part of the event).

Levels 1–7 build ideas and their organization in events such as descriptions, instructions, retellings, reports and stories. Levels 8–14 develop the basic narrative structures in more sophisticated activities such as presenting an argument for change, interviewing to gain specific information, or giving a public presentation.

The focus in teaching is on exchanging comments about what is happening to facilitate knowledge and understanding. This is in contrast to many situations, such as the teaching of reading, which are geared to obtaining skills. The COGS takes a very different approach, focusing on the multiple ways in which communication takes place. Two devices are promoted in the activities:

◆ **information-gap** experiences, such as guessing games and problem-solving tasks, which force participants to exchange information to find a solution

◆ **opinion-gap** experiences, which are created from controversial ideas, encouraging participants to share feelings, describe events and defend views.

The approach is based on knowledge about narrative structure, emphasizing that language is a tool used in discourse but that possessing it does not automatically mean you can communicate successfully (Westby, 1984). What is important is the ability to see behind, beyond and between words and thread together the meaning of events from an understanding of the underlying narrative structure. Narrative has a developmental basis that starts with a heap of ideas and develops into descriptions, instructions, explanations, reports and stories. The scheme starts with an initial diagnostic session, which allows the facilitator to decide the level to be taught, and after 8–10 hours' teaching in a small group participants are assessed on core and specific competencies. The experience focuses on both the process and product of learning and has had great success with many different groups of people, both children and adults.

◆ Circle time

The circle time method (Mosley, 1996) involves regular meetings for which children and staff sit together in an inclusive arrangement such as a circle. During the meetings, participants have the opportunity to speak about their feelings and concerns, and learn to collaborate in activities that aim to build co-operation and self-esteem. Trew (1999) has carried out a survey of 161 schools trained in the method and, although no hard evidence was produced, references in Ofsted findings have suggested that this is a powerful tool for dealing with social and emotional problems in school.

The approach has a freer framework than COGS and concentrates on the process rather than the specific products of learning. It allows students to control the action of events and gives them chances to express their views and feelings. In this sense it is very much in line with the COGS philosophy. The scheme is not built on a theory of communication and thinking like the COGS and does not attempt to measure progress against criteria in the same way. Nevertheless, it is a popular approach that children enjoy and teachers deem to be a benefit to their development.

◆ Nurture groups

The Green Paper *Excellence for All Children* (DfEE, 1997) highlights nurture groups as a promising intervention for early years children with emotional and behavioural difficulties.

Nurture groups (Boxall, 1996) are classes for 10–12 students, which are staffed by a teacher and teaching assistant. They are run on principles derived from attachment theory. This theory suggests that the earliest patterns of interactions between parent and infant seem to be a kind of 'dance' in which the child signals with smiles, cuddles, mutual gaze and cries, and the parent responds appropriately. The parents' attachment to the child may be affected by the ability of the pair to achieve an effective communication exchange.

There are clear sequences in the development of attachments, particularly in young infants, who go from diffuse attachment to a single attachment, and then to multiple attachments. In older children, there is a shift away from immature dependent behaviours, such as clinging or touching and holding, towards more mature forms, such as seeking attention and approval. Children differ in the strength and quality of their early attachments and in the speed with which they pass from the less to the more mature forms of dependency. Consistency in dependent behaviour throughout their lifetime is, however, more notable in females than males. Individual differences in attachment are partly determined by the primary caregiver's childcare practices, although the child's temperament may be influential too. Among older children the degree of dependency seems to be determined jointly by the amounts of reward and punishment that parents provide in response to the child's bid for dependency.

Nurture groups are built on the premise that attachments have not been properly developed in some children, which consequently affects their behaviour. The aim is to develop communication and behaviour through small-group teaching, and the focus is on the interaction between the child, adults and peers in an environment that is as home-like as possible. A feature of nurture groups is meeting at table for breakfast, and children engage in making preparations for this and clearing up afterwards, which fosters not only collaboration and co-operation skills but also communicative exchanges between individuals. The children follow the standard curriculum, but in a less pressured way; they usually attend the nurture group, which is part of the school, for about two terms before being integrated back into their class. The aim is to promote inclusion of children with emotional and behavioural difficulties into the mainstream.

A recent survey has suggested that nurture groups are a very effective method of helping children achieve. An assessment based on the Boxall profile of development (Boxall, 1996) is used to select students who will benefit from the approach.

◆ The Critical Skills Programme

The Critical Skills Programme, *Education by Design* (Mobilia and co-workers, 2001), is a classroom dynamic that guides thoughtful planning of learning experiences for students. It has two major tenets:

- ◆ problem-based learning
- ◆ collaborative learning communities.

In the programme, students and teachers work collaboratively to achieve desired results as they develop knowledge, understanding, critical skills and vital habits of mind. It is a set of tools and strategies for being purposeful in the process of engaging students in their learning, making the class run more smoothly and addressing learning goals that focus on quality work. At another level, the programme designs learning environments in a way that encourages results and honours democratic practices, collaborative working and student responsibility for learning. It is a model for transforming education in the reconstructionist philosophy, focusing less on teaching and more on learning, drawing on what we know about best practice.

The four ideas about education

Four broad ideas provide the building blocks for engaging students in their learning.

1. **Experiential learning** creates an environment that allows students to interact in real-life contexts, to construct individual meanings and engage in complex actions that reflect life outside school.

2. **Collaborative learning communities** comprise an intentionally structured classroom culture in which teachers and students support one another in pursuit of clearly articulated goals.

3. **Standards-driven learning** engages students in thoughtfully designed experiences that ensure they develop and practise the characteristics that foster knowledge, understanding and skills.

4. **Problem-based learning** is the use of challenges as the primary instructional approach; problems are posed for students to solve as individuals, in small groups, or within the full learning community.

The four ideas work together to form a coherent approach and a classroom culture of shared ideas so that students are able to meet targeted standards.

The ideas behind the Critical Skills Programme were developed at Antioch University in the USA (www.edbydesign.org) but were brought to Britain by Network Educational Press, who co-ordinate training in the method. (See also Weatherley (2000), Weatherley and co-workers (2002) and www.criticalskills.co.uk.) The training may be accredited towards the MA programme at the University of Leicester. The Level 1 and 2 coaching kit, *Education by Design: Critical Skills: Level 1 and Level 2* by Wendy Mobilia and co-workers (2001), is published by Network Educational Press.

Information processing quiz

How do you learn best – through your eyes, your ears or your sense of touch or body position?

Complete the quiz below and find out!

1 You are out walking – what do you notice first?

    A   other people, transport, buildings, animals

    B   people talking, cars hooting, music playing

    C   the heat, wind, rain

2 When you are annoyed do you …

    A   look someone in the eye defiantly?

    B   shout and scream?

    C   stamp your feet and make physical gestures?

3 Which of the following do you prefer?

    A   reading

    B   listening to music

    C   making or doing things

4 When learning something new do you prefer to …

    A   memorize from written or drawn information?

    B   repeat facts out loud to yourself?

    C   write down what you are trying to learn?

Answers on next page.

◆ Answers

Do you have a preference for one mode? This may indicate your information processing preference.

Mostly A: visual (seeing)

Mostly B: auditory (hearing)

Mostly C: touch, feeling, spatial positioning

Solution to Miller's Puzzle

from L. Miller, 'Problem Solving Hypothesis Testing and Language Disorders', in G. P. Wallach and K. G. Butler (eds), Language Learning Disabilities in School-Age Children *(Baltimore, Maryland: Williams and Wilkins, 1984)*

Appendix 4

Common learning difficulties and medical conditions in children

◆ Able children

National Association for Gifted Children

0845 450 0221
www.nagcbritain.org.uk

Advisory Centre for Education

0808 800 5793
www.ace-ed.org.uk

Able children are also known as 'gifted and talented'. 'Gifted' refers to those with exceptional abilities, whereas 'talented' are those who have developed their potential to a superior level through education, training and practice. Many people, however, use the terms interchangeably. The outstanding potential of able children is in one or more of the following areas:

◆ intellectual ability
◆ creative ability
◆ particular academic ability in a subject area
◆ leadership
◆ a performing art
◆ a visual art.

Such people represent only the top 1–2 per cent of the population and many do not make the most of their potential because of lack of opportunity. Some children hide their abilities because they do not want to stand out from their peers.

Characteristics

- ◆ Outstanding skills in their specific context.
- ◆ Unusual dedication to the development of their abilities.
- ◆ Confident and self-motivated.

Management

There is an argument that able children should be considered to have special educational needs because, unless extra opportunities are provided, they may not develop their abilities to the full. Under the 1981 Education Act, a local education authority has a general duty to identify a child with special educational needs but able children are not defined in this legislation. They do, however, have quite specific needs, and in 2001 the Government recognized this with the setting up of a special academy for the gifted and talented at the University of Warwick. The needs of able children may be met in three ways:

1 **Segregation**: There are potential benefits of special schools or classes for able students. This has to be balanced against the problems of removing them from less able children. The able person will need to learn how to work with people of various abilities in life situations.

2 **Acceleration**: An able child may pass through the school system faster than age peers so they are faced with more stimulation and challenge. Since older children may have different attitudes and interests, which the able child does not share, this could lead to isolation.

3 **Enrichment**: The able child stays with peers, but is provided with challenging experiences through individual programmes and support teaching. This is easier to arrange for some subject areas than others and depends on the experience of staff. Although this system retains a child's contact with age peers it can cause resentment and feelings of difference and isolation. This is the most common approach, however, and may be the best compromise for most children.

It is important that able children are involved in self-directed thinking and communication so that they can operate confidently at high levels. The Communication Opportunity Group Scheme has been very successful with this particular sector, as some able children do have problems relating successfully to others. Although such students are well advanced in some abilities, their emotional development follows age and life experience; there may be a large difference between this aspect and their gifted areas, which can cause social problems.

TIPS:

- ◆ Make sure able children are properly extended, but do not hold them up as perfect examples of what to aim for as this will cause resentment among peers.
- ◆ Co-operate with parents and look for opportunities for extra development in the community.

132

- Everyone has some gift or talent – make sure this is discussed and accepted by class members.
- Use differentiation of resources and tasks to provide for needs in normal lessons.
- Provide emotional support with a teaching assistant, learning mentor or counsellor, so the child has opportunities to talk through needs and deal with frustrations.

Classroom organization

- Pair up the able child with another in the class or school for support.
- Use the child's gifts for the benefit of others, while emphasizing all children's abilities.
- Discuss with the child their plans for development and how they can be met in and outside school.
- Provide support in a Communication Opportunity Group Scheme that allows the child to develop high levels of thinking and expression, in a format where they can choose the content and feel extended.

◆ Asthma

National Asthma Campaign

020 7226 2260
www.asthma.org.uk

Asthma is a common disease, in which the circular, smooth muscles of the branching air tubes of the lungs (bronchi) are narrowed as a result of their tightening (bronchospasm). It is easier to breathe in than out, the lungs becoming inflated and not easily emptied. A wheeze on breathing out is the most recognizable symptom. Sufferers are worse when levels of pollution are high, but it is not clear if this is the cause. The commonest type is allergic asthma, but it can be induced by infection, emotion, occupation and exertion. It is thought that 1 in 7 children are affected.

Characteristics

- Wheeze or chronic cough.
- Reaction to damp, mould, food additives, pollen and spores, fur and feathers.
- Cyanosis (blue skin) occurs if there is inadequate oxygen to the tissues.
- Attacks last for a few minutes or several hours.

Management

Asthma is treated using two types of medicine: *relievers* and *preventers*. Both medicines come in small packs called inhalers or puffers, and each needs to be breathed in deeply, but they work in different ways. Reliever medicines help symptoms by relaxing muscles around the airways, so they open to make breathing easier. Reliever inhalers are normally blue in colour and must always be carried on the person. Preventer medicines calm inflamed airways and stop irritation, so reducing the risk of an attack. Effects build over time and the medicine must be taken daily.

TIP:

◆ If a child has an asthmatic attack, stay calm as anxiety can aggravate the condition.
◆ Reassure the child, but do not put an arm around him as this may increase spasms.
◆ Make sure the inhaler is used correctly.
◆ Encourage the child to sit upright and lean forward.
◆ Loosen clothing and offer a drink of tepid water.
◆ Call medical help if an attack lasts more than 5–10 minutes, checking the child uses the inhaler every few minutes until the doctor or ambulance arrives.

Classroom organization

◆ Make sure all staff are aware of what to do in case of an attack.
◆ Reduce risk factors in class and keep the child indoors if the pollution level or pollen count is high.
◆ Ensure the class is warm but airy.
◆ Ensure the child warms up gently for PE lessons.
◆ Watch the child in cold, dry weather as this triggers an attack.
◆ Ensure the child gets plenty of exercise, using the inhaler beforehand to prevent problems.

◆ Attention deficit hyperactivity disorder (ADHD)

ADDNet

ADDNet is the UK's national website for attention deficit hyperactivity disorder: www.btinternet.com/~black.ice/addnet/

The term 'attention deficit hyperactivity disorder' defines overactive, impulsive children who have difficulty in paying attention. If lack of attention is more evident, the description 'attention deficit disorder' (ADD) is used. Associated factors are neurological damage or underdevelopment, diet and poor socialization. About 1:100 of children may be affected and five times more boys than girls are reported with this condition.

Characteristics

◆ Restless and unable to sit still.

◆ Interferes with other children's activities.

◆ Runs about inappropriately.

◆ Fails to wait or turn take.

◆ Acts impulsively.

◆ Distracted and forgetful.

◆ Difficulty in completing tasks.

◆ Fails to listen and follow instructions.

◆ Interrupts others and cannot stop talking.

◆ Blurts out answers without being asked.

Management

◆ **Diet** eliminating salicylates, found in some fruit and vegetables, flavourings and preservatives, helps hyperactive children with food intolerances.

◆ **Medication** such as methylphenidate (Ritalin) dampens down behaviour but is controversial because it slows learning and benefits lessen over time.

◆ **Behaviour therapy** views that faulty learning, during socialization, can be unlearned.

◆ **Biofeedback** uses a self-monitoring instrument, which responds to the relevant behaviour, by emitting a sound when it is produced. In hyperactivity, muscle tension is measured. When it is too high, the sound reminds the child to relax and control the behaviour.

TIPS:

◆ Keep calm, as anger will be mirrored in the child.

◆ Find ways to distract.

◆ Provide clear, consistent rules, routines and responsibilities.

◆ Warn when something is about to happen or finish.

◆ Make eye contact before speaking, otherwise you will be ignored.

◆ Keep instructions simple – one per sentence.

◆ Provide choice, to avoid a 'no' response; for example, 'Do you want to do your homework in the lunch break or at home?'

◆ Use a 'time out' strategy to deal with tantrums.

◆ Give specific praise for appropriate behaviour.

135

Classroom organization

- ◆ Arrange the classroom to minimize distractions.
- ◆ Set short, achievable targets with rewards for completion.
- ◆ Alternate active and passive tasks, using constant variety.
- ◆ Present texts with large, well-spaced formats.
- ◆ Rehearse class rules, routines and responsibilities regularly.
- ◆ Provide checklists as a framework for completing tasks.
- ◆ Encourage the child to verbalize tasks, first to the teacher and then to himself.
- ◆ Praise before suggesting improvements: 'You've written interesting things. Next time, try to keep your words on the line as you write.'
- ◆ Give responsibilities, so others can view the child positively and boost self-esteem.

◆ Autistic spectrum disorders (ASD) – Autism

National Autistic Society

020 7833 2299
www.nas.org.uk

Centre for the Study of Autism

www.autism.org

Autism is the inability to make sense of the world. The condition was identified by Leo Kanner, an American psychiatrist, in the 1940s. It may also be called Kanner syndrome or childhood schizophrenia. It is thought to be the result of organic brain damage, with an estimated prevalence of 1:100, affecting four times as many boys as girls. About 80 per cent of autistic people have learning difficulties and a third have epileptic fits at some time. Some have an exceptional talent in an area not requiring social understanding (for example, maths, music, art and so on). Up to 10 per cent will become independent adults, with about 30 per cent needing some support and the rest requiring lifelong help.

Characteristics: a triad of impairments

- ◆ **Social interaction** – difficulties in understanding and interpreting social situations, displaying inappropriate and odd behaviours and an unwillingness to make friends.
- ◆ **Communication** – difficulties in making sense of and using both verbal and non-verbal information. Some use language but interpret it over-literally, while others never develop speech. Talk tends to involve repetition of learned phrases and is often inappropriate for the situation.

◆ **Thought and imagination** – difficulties in thinking flexibly and changing mental set for a new task. Responses are repetitive and obsessive, with fixation on certain objects and little development in play.

May demonstrate:

◆ Sensitivity to any stimuli.

◆ Aggressive behaviour.

◆ Hyperactivity.

◆ Self-injury.

◆ Hand-flapping, rocking or spinning movements.

◆ Strange eating habits.

◆ Odd gait or posture – such as walking on tip-toe.

◆ Fears or phobias.

Management

◆ Work on social communication; the Communication Opportunity Group Scheme has been successful with this group (Nelson and Burchell, 1998).

◆ Control inappropriate behaviours using behavioural techniques.

◆ Recognize that literal understanding means that autistics do not generalize learning easily, so it is important to teach carefully how to respond in all situations.

TIPS:

◆ Be calm, flexible, positive and patient.

◆ Provide clear boundaries for behaviour and prepare for changes in advance.

◆ Communicate constantly with parents and have high expectations.

◆ Disapprove of inappropriate behaviour, not of the child.

◆ Teach recognition of emotions, behaviours and body language.

◆ Do not expect eye contact and never turn the child's face to look at you.

◆ Refer to the child by name – she will probably not realize that 'everyone' includes her.

◆ Keep verbal instructions short and simple.

◆ Teach social interaction through activities and stories.

◆ Teach jokes, puns and metaphors.

◆ Use computers, as they are not emotionally demanding.

◆ Develop a buddy system as a way to provide support and help social development.

Classroom organization

- ◆ Structure the classroom with specific, labelled areas for tasks.
- ◆ Acknowledge the need for personal space by providing an individual work area.
- ◆ Use a visual timetable and task lists.
- ◆ Minimize noise and harsh lighting.
- ◆ Introduce one skill at a time and use visual prompts.
- ◆ Provide clear, consistent routines and minimize changes, as these upset such students.
- ◆ Make sure that everyone who comes into contact with the child knows how to react to him.

◆ Autistic spectrum disorders (ASD) — Asperger syndrome (AS)

National Autistic Society

020 7833 2299

www.nas.org.uk

Asperger Syndrome Education Network

www.aspennj.org

Asperger syndrome is regarded by some as a distinctive condition, but by others as the higher-ability end of the autistic spectrum. Causes are thought to be neuro-biological triggers that affect brain development. Suggested numbers are up to 1:250 with more males than females affected. The disorder is characterized by the same triad of impairments as autism, but these are less profound. Such children find it hard to interact successfully with others and make friends. Although they can speak fluently, they tend to be poor listeners, appearing insensitive to others. AS children demonstrate the same literal understanding as autistics. While often excelling at learning facts and figures, people with AS have problems thinking in abstract ways and find literature and religious studies difficult to grasp. Tips and class management strategies are the same as for the autistic child.

◆ Brittle bones

Brittle Bones Association

01382 204446

www.brittlebone.org

This is a genetic disorder known medically as osteogenesis imperfecta (OI). It refers to a range of conditions resulting from abnormalities in the protein structure of the bones, which causes a tendency for them to break easily. It is not caused by lack of calcium. Mild forms are usually inherited, but others happen out of the blue because of a genetic mutation. As the genetic effect is dominant, a carrier has a 50 per cent chance of passing on the condition to his or her children. About 1:20,000 babies are born annually with the disease. There is no cure but treatment is improving.

Characteristics

- ◆ Some children with brittle bones are of normal stature but fragile, while others are small and unable to walk.
- ◆ Up to 100 fractures in childhood lead to delays in the development of large-scale body movements such as walking.
- ◆ Fractures happen in normal activities, such as closing a door.
- ◆ Adolescents do not fracture as easily.
- ◆ Lax joints and muscles lead to fine motor problems.
- ◆ Often use left hand, even though naturally right-handed, because the right hand suffers more breaks.
- ◆ May have triangular-shaped faces.
- ◆ May face progressive limb deformities and chronic bone pain.
- ◆ Respiratory problems occur, because of underdeveloped lungs.

TIPS:

- ◆ Talk to child and parents about helpful routines.
- ◆ Get advice from a physiotherapist or occupational therapist about adaptations and equipment needed at each stage of education.
- ◆ Make use of adapted keyboards and voice-activated software if hand movements are restricted.
- ◆ Use a sloped desk for handwriting and different sizes or shapes of pen.
- ◆ Arrange seating so that the child is not crowded and others will not bump him.
- ◆ Provide handouts or copies of notes if writing is very difficult.
- ◆ Provide a dictaphone to use for recording information.
- ◆ Provide a cue card to call for help.

Classroom organization

◆ Make sure all staff and students are aware of the condition and how to help.

◆ Talk about the problems in PSHE, if the child and parents are willing.

◆ Allow the child to leave class early and get to the next place without pressure.

◆ Use a buddy system for support.

◆ Provide pastoral support, particularly as the child gets older.

◆ Ensure liaison between school, home and hospital.

◆ Organize home tuition when necessary.

◆ Plan for missed time because of broken limbs.

◆ Plan ahead for transfers.

◆ Encourage out-of-school activities, as social isolation is common.

◆ Expect high academic standards, as children with this condition are generally of normal intelligence.

◆ Treat as normally as possible, to ensure healthy emotional development.

◆ Encourage independence.

◆ Games are not recommended, but include swimming as exercise and any other non-weight-bearing activity.

◆ Make school safe, but do not be held responsible for breaks on the premises, as they can occur in normal activity such as getting up from a chair.

◆ Cerebral palsy (CP)

Scope

0808 800 3333

www.scope.org.uk

The National Institute of Conductive Education

0121 449 1569

www.conductive-education.org.uk

Inclusive Technology Ltd

01457 819790

www.inclusive.co.uk

SEMERC Information Service, Granada Learning

0161 827 2719

www.granada-learning.com/semercindex

The term 'cerebral palsy' defines a wide range of non-progressive brain disorders of posture and movement. Brain damage happens before or after birth (for example, infections or strangulation by the umbilical cord). Difficulties with vision, hearing, thinking and speaking are common and about one-third experience epileptic seizures.

Types and characteristics (forms often co-exist)

Spastic means *stiff*, with sufferers having stiffened muscles and decreased joint movements, due to cerebral cortex damage. (Three quarters of the CP population fall into this category.)

- Hemiplegia – one side of the body affected.
- Diplegia – legs affected more than arms.
- Quadriplegia – arms and legs affected.

Athetoid defines a rapid change from floppy to tense muscles, resulting in writhing, involuntary movements, because of damage to the basal ganglia.

Ataxic sufferers have difficulty with balance and poor spatial awareness, due to damage in the cerebellum. Sufferers walk unsteadily and have shaky, jerky movements. This is a rare form.

Management

Although there is no cure for this non-progressive disorder, posture and muscle control can be improved by physiotherapy, perception and spatial awareness by occupational therapy and communication by speech and language therapy. Those with severe forms of movement disturbance will need computerized aids to communicate. Teachers must be aware of how to position CP children correctly, otherwise they will be unable to function. Close co-operation with therapists is essential. Many children who are regarded as clumsy will be at the low end of the CP continuum. Although they might not have consulted medical specialists, they will benefit from help to improve balance, posture and movement co-ordination.

TIPS:
- Remember that someone with severe physical impairments may have above average intelligence.
- Promote understanding of the student's needs through subject areas such as PSHE.
- Communicate with parents and other experts involved with the child, for correct handling.
- Co-ordinate work of therapists – to be aware of breathing, feeding, posture and movement techniques.
- Pair up the student with a suitable buddy, but make sure the buddy is not overburdened.
- Make use of ICT, especially for communication. Inclusive Technology and SEMERC are specialist providers (see opposite).
- Use audio-visual aids as support.

Classroom organization

- ◆ Ensure physical access – ramps, toilets, classroom layout.
- ◆ Make sure a teaching assistant is well trained in the use of aids, such as head pointers, individualized wheelchairs, electronic devices and adaptive equipment.
- ◆ Clarify associated difficulties, such as visual perception, hearing, and so on.
- ◆ Ensure the student is in a good position to view class activities, because she will not be able to adjust herself to hear and see like others.
- ◆ Work on class understanding of differences and how to accommodate these.

◆ Communication disorders: speech, language and social use [semantic-pragmatics]

Human Communication International

www.hci.org.uk   email: rs70@leicester.ac.uk

Afasic – speech, language and communication

020 7490 9410
www.afasic.org.uk

ICAN – helping children to communicate

0845 225 4071
www.ican.org.uk

SMIRA – Selective Mutism Information and Research Association

0116 270 7705 or 0116 212 7411

There are many aspects of communication problems, ranging from understanding and using verbal and non-verbal forms, to moving the muscles that control speaking. Up to 10 per cent of children have significant deficits and 50 per cent of children and adults do not use communication effectively for work and social exchanges. Causes may be genetic flaws, biological disturbances such as hearing loss or cleft palate, injury or illness, general learning problems or environmental issues such as lack of opportunity and inadequate stimulation.

Aspects and characteristics

- ◆ **Speech apparatus** includes mouth, tongue, lips, nose, muscles and breathing. Incorrect or inefficient functioning leads to impairment such as dysfluency (stammering).
- ◆ **Phonology** refers to the sounds that make up language; problems are demonstrated in vowel and consonant errors.

◆ **Grammar** refers to word functions such as nouns, verbs, adjectives, adverbs, conjunctions and connectives. Problems are seen in the selection of the wrong form (for example, 'I runny' for 'I am running' – adjectival form used instead of verb).

◆ **Syntax** is the way words and sentences are put together in conventional subject–verb–object relationships (for example, 'I [subject] went running [verb] in the mountains [object]'). Difficulties are evident in the muddled use of these patterns (for example, 'Running I mountains went').

◆ **Semantics** refers to word meanings. The common 500 words have approximately 15,000 different meanings. Take the word 'run' – you can easily find 30 applications for this! Problems are common in mathematics, when children do not grasp that everyday words (for example, 'take away') have another use in numerical calculations.

◆ **Pragmatics** refers to the way in which verbal and non-verbal language is used to express feelings and ideas in different contexts. Common problems involve inappropriate use for a situation because the clues and nuances of the exchange are not noticed and understood. Because this problem involves thinking ability, such children cannot cope with abstract concepts such as 'imagine', 'guess' and 'next', often appearing stupid, rude, arrogant, gauche and over-sensitive or insensitive to situations.

◆ **Prosody** refers to the intonation and stress (rhythm) of speech. Problems are seen in the lack of use of voice dynamics – pitch, pace, pause, power and pronunciation. Speech is commonly too fast or slow and monotonous in tone. As we mark meaning with these dynamics, lack of use in one's own speech is reflected in poor understanding of others.

Management

Children have two broad categories of difficulty; they may have problems being:

◆ **receptive** – understanding the meaning of what others say and do

◆ **expressive** – using words, gestures (including eye contact and reference), movements, facial expressions, voice tone and social conventions, so others understand what they say and do.

Those with problems across the range of aspects could be within the autistic spectrum, as these people have difficulty processing all the information from a situation and responding appropriately. Children, with either specific problems or delayed development, will need advice and input from a speech and language therapist and, in school, would benefit from the support of a Communication Opportunity Group Scheme. Do not expect spontaneous or generalized learning; these children are hard work but are rewarding.

As education centres on communication, any impairment will affect cognitive, emotional and social skills. Assessment of communication requires a clear, structural model such as categories of reception and expression. Difficulties may also be structured according to mode of transmission – speech, print or gesture (including sign language). An example of speech impairment would be a stammer; a disorder involving print would be dyslexia. Dyspraxia demonstrates a problem in carrying out a pattern of movement, despite the person understanding what is required and being physically able to comply. An aspect of dyspraxia may be deficits in speech co-ordination, in which sounds can be made, but not under conscious control to form words.

143

Another classification of disorders is *organic* and *functional*.

- ◆ Organic problems have an explicit medical cause, and include conditions such as aphasia, caused by damage to, or abnormality of, the cerebral cortex. Receptive aphasia is lack of understanding, whereas expressive aphasia is an inability to form ideas and put them into words.

- ◆ Functional disorders have no clear medical pathology and include some examples of dyslexia, where no brain abnormalities are demonstrated.

Yet another distinction is between *delay* and *deviance*.

- ◆ Delay refers to a normal pattern which is slow to develop.

- ◆ Deviance signifies abnormal growth features.

TIPS:

- ◆ Use short, simple, specific sentences with good pauses between them to give time for processing (for example, 'Put books and pencils in your work trays' rather than 'Tidy up').
- ◆ Always check for understanding and define unfamiliar words.
- ◆ Supplement speech with appropriate gestures, movements and visual props.
- ◆ Make your voice expressive and interesting to listen to.
- ◆ Give time to reply after a question.
- ◆ Interpret what the child means, rather than accept what he says when it does not make sense.
- ◆ Explain jokes, metaphors and sarcasm, as these are not automatically understood.
- ◆ Teach idiomatic expressions and appropriate language and behaviour for different situations.

Classroom organization

- ◆ Reduce the amount of passive listening, and plan lessons involving plenty of active participation.

- ◆ Provide a quiet, orderly working environment.

- ◆ Make rules, routines and responsibilities clear, constantly reviewing and displaying these for regular reference.

- ◆ Provide reminders, supported by task lists and pictures, diagrams or symbols.

- ◆ Keep to class routines and explain changes in advance. Spell out how they will affect students, so they know explicitly how they need to respond.

- ◆ Encourage visualizing, so the student learns to create moving pictures in her head of what is said.

- ◆ Provide opportunities to learn how to communicate in social situations, through the Communication Opportunity Group Scheme, for example.

◆ Make sure the child has individual talk time with an adult (for example, teaching assistant, learning mentor or counsellor), so he can be specifically coached to perform better.

◆ Be aware that misunderstandings lead to behaviour and social problems.

◆ Liaise with parents and other professionals, so there is consistent management of problems.

◆ Diabetes

Diabetes UK

020 7424 1030

www.diabetes.org.uk

Diabetes mellitus is a condition in which the amount of glucose (sugar) in the blood can get too high (or too low) because the body cannot use it properly. The hormone insulin, made by the pancreas, normally controls glucose levels but in people with diabetes the pancreatic cells either do not make enough or the insulin they make does not work. There are around 1.5 million sufferers in the UK, with a further 1 million undiagnosed. The incidence of the condition among school children is 1:700, with both sexes equally affected. There is a strong heredity factor.

Types and characteristics

◆ Type 1 diabetes occurs when there is a severe lack of insulin, due to destruction of cells in the pancreas. It is common in children and sufferers under 40 years of age. Symptoms appear quickly and are obvious. Treatment is by insulin injection and managed diet. Most have injections twice daily.

◆ Type 2 diabetes occurs when the pancreas cannot produce sufficient insulin, or when the insulin that is produced does not work properly, and is common in the over forties. Diet alone, diet plus tablets, or diet and injections, are used for treatment depending on severity. Development is slow and symptoms are less severe than for Type 1. It is often unnoticed because symptoms are put down to age or over-work!

Symptoms

◆ Increased thirst.

◆ Increased urination.

◆ Extreme tiredness.

◆ Weight loss.

◆ Genital itching.

◆ Blurred vision.

If blood sugar becomes too low, a person may develop hypoglycaemia and become unconscious (diabetic coma). If blood sugar is too high, sufferers can develop hyperglycaemia. The first condition is more common in schools, and can be caused by missing snacks or meals, extra exercise, too much insulin or weather extremes.

Management

Medical assessment aims to find a satisfactory regime to control the condition. A sensible lifestyle with regular, nutritious food, proper sleep, rest and exercise, reduces serious health problems later, such as heart disease.

TIPS:

- Be aware of symptoms: hunger, sweating, drowsiness, pallor, glazed eyes, shaking, mood changes (especially aggression) and lack of concentration.
- Communicate with the child and parents regularly, to update on treatment procedures.
- In the case of adverse reactions to low glucose levels, give fast-acting sugar to raise blood levels: sugary drinks (but not diet versions), mini chocolate bar, fresh fruit juice, glucose tablets, jam or honey, for example. If the child is too confused to help himself, rub jam or honey on the inside of the cheek.
- Keep 'emergency supplies' in the teacher's desk and check the child has some sugary food in his pocket.
- When the child recovers from an episode, he needs a slow-reacting starchy food, such as a sandwich. He is likely to feel tired, nauseous and have a headache.
- In the rare event of a child becoming unconscious, call an ambulance without delay.

Classroom organization

- Make sure all staff know the symptoms and can take prompt action using an agreed routine.
- For a younger diabetic child, allow regular visits to the toilet.
- Help a younger child develop a routine for timing their food, explaining the situation to class mates so everyone understands that she is not eating out of turn.
- Allow the diabetic child to be first in lunch queues.
- Adolescents commonly rebel against the strict management regime and may need counselling.
- Regular exercise helps to prevent problems.

◆ Down's syndrome

The Down's Syndrome Association

020 8682 4001

www.downs-syndrome.org.uk

Down's syndrome is a genetic disorder, resulting from an additional chromosome (47 instead of 46). There are around 300 distinguishing characteristics, among the most obvious of which are reduced stature, a flat nasal bridge, small mouth, protruding tongue and transverse single palmar creases on the hand. There is a high incidence of heart problems, bowel malformations, predispositions to infections, leukaemia and learning difficulties. It occurs in 2:1,000 births and results in delayed development. More boys are affected than girls.

Characteristics

- ◆ Delayed gross and fine motor skills.
- ◆ Hearing and vision impairments.
- ◆ Speech and language impairments.
- ◆ Sequencing problems.
- ◆ Limited auditory memory.
- ◆ Limited concentration span.
- ◆ Problems in thinking and reasoning and applying knowledge to new situations.
- ◆ Often happy and sociable.

Management

There is no definite guide to management and people are confused about how to handle people with Down's syndrome. They look physically different and used to be referred to as Mongol, because flat features resemble those of the Mongolian race. There is a wide variety of ability among this group. Many people with Down's syndrome grow up to lead independent lives, holding down jobs and enjoying lasting relationships. There are examples of Down's syndrome students achieving well in higher education.

TIPS:

- ◆ Nominate a key person in school to be the point of contact to sort out difficulties.
- ◆ Teach routines and rules, constantly reviewing these.
- ◆ Make sure the student has a clear timetable, to refer to regularly.
- ◆ Attend to the development of communication, as this is generally a problem.

147

- ◆ Use short, simple sentences.
- ◆ Speak directly to the student, reinforcing words with facial expressions and gestures.
- ◆ Give time for processing information and responding.
- ◆ Provide extra practice for motor skills.
- ◆ Consider if inappropriate behaviour results from lack of understanding, reaction to tasks that are too easy, difficult or lengthy, or materials that are unsuitable, for example.

Classroom organization

- ◆ If one-to-one support is provided, make sure this does not prevent contact with other students.
- ◆ Ensure the student works with good role models for communication and behaviour.
- ◆ Ensure consistent approaches among all who work with the student.
- ◆ Provide activity boxes, giving extra practice for fine motor skills, when the student finishes a task before peers.
- ◆ Set up listening and talk activities with others.
- ◆ Make sure differences are discussed positively in PSHE lessons.

◆ Dyscalculia

The Dyscalculia Site

www.dyscalculia.org.uk

Dyscalculia is a specific learning difficulty with mathematics. Possible causes are faults in foetal development, preventing correct wiring up of the brain, fear, inadequate instruction or all three.

Types and characteristics

Developmental dyscalculia occurs when there is a marked discrepancy between general developmental level and measures of mathematics ability.

Dyscalculia itself is a total inability to understand and use number concepts, characterized by the following.

- ◆ Inability to count by rote.
- ◆ Difficulty reading and/or writing numbers.
- ◆ Inconsistent computation performances.
- ◆ Omissions, reversals and transpositions of numbers.

- Limited mental mathematics ability.
- Inability to grasp and remember mathematical concepts, rules and formulae.
- Difficulty with time and time management.
- Problems with sequencing, including team games and dance sequences.
- Poor directional sense.
- Poor memory for layout.
- Confusion of left and right.
- Stress at lesson change-over times.
- Inability to remember names or faces.
- Difficulties with handling money.

TIPS:

- Find out what type of learner the student is and use her preferences.
- Encourage the student to use rough paper for workings and explain answers.
- Use clear steps to explain a new idea.
- Encourage the student to teach the new idea back, to check understanding.
- Use concrete materials, pictures and other visual stimuli.
- Use multisensory approaches – for example, a sand tray for tracing number shapes.
- Teach the language of mathematics.
- Use number stories to build narrative thinking and structure.
- Make sure work is not cluttered on a page.
- Encourage use of calculators to speed the calculation process.

Classroom organization

- Use wall displays to reinforce ideas – the four symbols (+, –, ×, ÷) and all the words that represent them.
- Encourage peer support in lessons and from one lesson to another.
- Acknowledge the trauma such students face, by programming a check-in slot where they can express anxieties and review progress.
- Provide credit card holders for reminders of tables and formulae
- Teach with mnemonics (for example, 'the octopus octagon').
- Make sure help is available for tests and exams and allow dyscalculic students extra time.

◆ Dyslexia

The British Dyslexia Association

0118 966 8271
www.bda-dyslexia.org.uk

Dyslexia Institute

01784 222300
www.dyslexia-inst.org.uk

Dyslexia, in literal translation, means 'difficulty with words' and is the inability to reach expected standards in reading, writing and spelling. It is regarded as a complex neurological condition affecting up to 10 per cent of people, predominantly boys.

Characteristics

- ◆ Slow information processing for spoken and written language.
- ◆ Limited short-term memory.
- ◆ Sequencing and organizational difficulties.
- ◆ Tiredness.
- ◆ Uneven performances.
- ◆ Frustration may lead to bad behaviour.

Reading is slow, so there are problems in gaining an overall meaning of the content. Many dyslexics describe print as swirling and have tracking difficulties, frequently losing their place. They experience problems in blending and segmenting sounds in words due to inadequate phonological processing. They make constant errors with high frequency words ('and', 'the', 'but' and so on) but often cope better with more difficult words as these are more easily visualized.

Writing is normally of an inadequate standard, displaying letter confusions and distortions ('tired' for 'tried' and so on). Spelling is often bizarre and work very messy.

Management

Dyslexics are often good lateral thinkers and do well in right-brain activities such as art, drama and sport. They benefit from an oral-to-literate approach, developing and organizing ideas first through talk, before putting them into written form. Similarly, with reading dyslexics are helped by talking about the story and gaining an overview of the meaning, before attempting to decode the words. Reading through action rhymes is often successful; they learn to integrate sound and movement before mapping on to the written word the sequence already established. It is essential to develop visualization techniques (Sage, 2003).

TIPS:

- Work from strong skills.
- Use a judicial multisensory approach as outlined above.
- Use pictures, flow charts and plans, visualizing and talking about ideas before reading or writing about them.
- Use audio tapes for the student to record information before writing it.
- ICT and voice recognition software is helpful.
- Employ coloured overlays, line trackers and bookmarks, if they help.
- Allow time for tasks and give constant praise for efforts.
- Encourage the student to keep a notebook of words required for writing in subject lessons, and to learn these using a 'look, copy, cover and recall' strategy. This is often more successful than a structured spelling programme, as words are needed and used constantly, providing natural repetition and motivation to learn. A thesaurus, from the age of about eight years, is a real boon.

Classroom organization

- Provide a memory map of the lesson, which is available afterwards on a wall display.
- Teach study skills, as these are vital for dyslexics and helpful to the whole class.
- Reduce board work to a minimum and never ask the dyslexic to copy from this.
- Make sure that tests are short and frequent rather than long and occasional.
- Provide extra help for tests and exams and arrange for extra time for the dyslexic student.
- Allow work on computer (a small laptop, for example), to help the student keep up with peers.
- Provide oral tests, as well as written, as dyslexics do better in these.
- Provide extra help, such as a Communication Opportunity Group Scheme, which allows students to develop thinking, processing and expressing skills in both speech and writing.

◆ Dyspraxia

Dyspraxia Foundation

www.dyspraxiafoundation.org.uk

Dyspraxia is a motor impairment, in which a person is unable to perform purposive movements, although he is not paralysed or deficient in muscle co-ordination. The cause is an immaturity in processing information, so that messages are not transmitted properly. There may be problems in co-ordinating fine and gross movements, perception and thought. About 1:20 of the population are affected, with four times as many boys as girls reported with the condition.

Characteristics

- ◆ Delayed development, such as crawling, walking and talking.
- ◆ Problems understanding spatial language: 'in', 'on', 'in front', 'behind' and so on.
- ◆ Problems following instructions.
- ◆ Limited concentration.
- ◆ Problems with laterality.
- ◆ Difficulty in picking up small objects and holding pencils, pens, paintbrushes and so on.
- ◆ Difficulty with jigsaws and sorting activities.
- ◆ Difficulty with dressing and eating.
- ◆ Difficulty with games, movement and music.
- ◆ Inability to recognize dangerous situations.
- ◆ Limited social skills.
- ◆ Poor posture and body awareness.
- ◆ Tiredness and irritability.

Management

Therapy (physio or occupational, and speech and language) is very necessary for these children as they need expert help in developing thinking and co-ordination, to provide a base for their learning. Teachers need advice on how to facilitate good posture, movement, perception, speech accuracy and fluency.

TIPS:

◆ Provide extra supervision and give encouragement to stay on task.

◆ Make instructions short and simple and check for understanding (note that dyspraxics do not understand sarcasm or irony).

◆ Limit handwriting and use a laptop to record, as writing is laborious.

◆ Break tasks into small steps.

◆ Use colour and chunking to aid in following text.

◆ Teach strategies to remember and facilitate self-organization.

◆ Understand that growth spurts accentuate basic movement problems.

Classroom organization

◆ Position the student where she has a direct view of the teacher and there are minimal distractions.

◆ Make sure seating allows the student to place both feet on the floor for postural stability. Provide a sloping surface, at elbow height, for work.

◆ Limit board work and copying from this, as it is impossible for dyspraxics to look, remember and write.

◆ Be aware of limitations in sport and movement activities, giving a role that allows success.

◆ Provide a buddy to help with tricky situations.

◆ Secure paper with tacky putty for writing or drawing.

◆ Keep in touch with parents and other professionals, such as therapists, for specific advice.

◆ Emotional and behavioural difficulties (EBD)

Centre for Studies on Inclusive Education

0117 344 4007
inclusion.uwe.ac.uk

Emotional and behavioural difficulties disrupt others and cause social and educational problems. There are various causes, such as abuse, neglect, physical or mental illness, sensory or physical impairment or psychological trauma. EBD refers to a range of difficulties, including neurosis, antisocial behaviour and psychosis. According to the Office for National Statistics, 10 per cent of children have a mental health disorder. The national children's mental health charity Young Minds believes up to 40 per cent of young people in inner cities have emotional and behaviour problems.

Types and characteristics
Neurosis

◆ Anxiety disorder (symptoms: sleeping problems, aches and pains).

◆ Phobia (irrational fear – dog phobias are common in children).

◆ Obsessive/compulsive behaviour (ritualistic, pointless routines that interfere with living).

◆ Avoidance/withdrawal (clinging, fearful, tearful and solitary).

◆ Hypochondria (worry about health).

◆ Hysteria (regress or lose memory).

◆ Depression (feelings of worthlessness shown in withdrawal).

◆ Eating/sleeping disorders, incontinence.

Antisocial behaviour [conduct disorder]

◆ Disruption (annoying behaviours).

◆ Aggression.

◆ Lack of co-operation.

◆ Delinquency.

Psychotic behaviour

◆ Schizophrenia (occurs in adolescence, characterized by thought disorders).

◆ Dementia (reduced intellectual abilities due to damage or deterioration in brain tissue).

◆ Toxic confusion (due to drug abuse or accidental poisoning, such as lead).

◆ Reactive psychosis (occurs in times of stress; sufferers demonstrate lack of contact with reality and bizarre behaviour).

Management

EBD responds to behaviour modification, psychotherapy, cognitive therapy and counselling from appropriately trained experts. Drugs may help depression and doctors suggest that about 10 per cent of children are now so stressed that they need medical support. The prognosis tends to be poorer for children with antisocial behaviour than for those with neurotic problems. Some children show more than one type of difficulty. Work with families and support in the community is essential. The majority of teachers feel that EBD children should be educated separately (Sage and Sommefeldt, 2004).

TIPS:

◆ Make rules and routines clear, and review them constantly.

◆ Organize a key person to keep in regular one-to-one contact and use him to develop behaviour targets with the student.

◆ Use circle time to gain peer support and discuss problems that disrupt the class.

◆ For younger children, explore the nurture group methods.

◆ Explore the Communication Opportunity Group Scheme, as experts think that many children have communication difficulties first and behaviour problems second.

◆ Enlist the support of parents and other colleagues to ensure consistent handling.

◆ Provide opportunities for expressive activities through art, drama, music and so on.

Classroom organization

◆ Make sure the student sits by good role models to help shape positive behaviour.

◆ Put rules, routines and responsibilities on posters for class display, drawing attention to these each lesson.

◆ Insecure children benefit from lesson overviews (in one school the key person sees the EBD student at the beginning of the day to chat through lessons and expectations).

◆ Always be firm, fair and sympathetic to the underlying problems.

◆ Arrange a space for 'time out', either inside or outside the class, if behaviour becomes too disruptive.

◆ Discuss, with the student, steps that will be taken to help with coping, such as 'time out', so it is understood that this is not so much a punishment as a strategy to help everyone.

◆ Keep in contact with parents and therapists to ensure co-operative management occurs.

◆ Epilepsy

Epilepsy Action

0808 800 5050
www.epilepsy.org.uk

Epilepsy results from a temporary change in the way brain cells work. Messages become scrambled, due to an upset in brain chemistry that causes neurons (brain cells) to fire off faster than normal. The electrical 'storm' that occurs triggers a seizure that interferes with normal functioning. There are forty different types of seizure caused by various chemical processes, sited in different areas of the brain.

The condition is the second most common neurological disorder after migraine and affects 1:130 people in the UK; 75 per cent of these have their first seizure before the age of 20. Epilepsy is common in teachers' experiences.

Types and characteristics

There are two main types of seizure.

◆ A **partial seizure** occurs when a specific part of the brain is affected, and the nature of a fit depends on brain area involved. The child will not pass out but consciousness will be affected.

◆ A **generalised seizure** affects a large part of the brain. Fits vary from major convulsive episodes, with unconsciousness and limb jerking, to momentary lapses and eyelid fluttering. These vary, therefore, from temporary absences, where a child appears daydreaming (*petit mal*), to full tonic seizures (*grand mal*).

Management

Treatment is normally by drugs that regulate the chemical processes in the brain, so allowing sufferers to lead normal lives. All drugs aim to prevent rather than treat seizures and must be taken on a daily basis to ensure this. They all cause side effects and have to be monitored and changed until the user finds the one that suits best. Possible side effects include dizziness, headaches, nausea, tiredness, memory limitations, slow reaction times and impaired motor control. If a child is constantly drowsy or over-active, it is indicative that drugs need adjusting, so always inform parents.

With adequate supervision there is no activity that needs to be barred, but if there is a history of frequent and unpredictable fits, it is wise to avoid climbing activities. Swimming is beneficial but make sure a buddy is always around in case of problems.

TIPS:

◆ Consider trigger factors and how to minimize these: stress, bright lights, lack of sleep or rest, illness, hormones, food (meals should not be skipped and good nutrition must be observed).
◆ Provide a calm, positive environment that reduces risks.
◆ Keep in touch with the child and parents to monitor any changes.
◆ Discuss the problem with classmates and enlist support to avoid teasing.
◆ Be alert for 'daydreamers', as they can miss out on learning.
◆ Allow for catching up missed work.
◆ Ensure school records have up-to-date details of medication, type of seizure and emergency plans.

Classroom organization

Make sure key personnel are trained in dealing with seizures. If a seizure occurs:

◆ do not hold the child down or stop him moving about

◆ put a cushion under the head and loosen clothing

◆ move furniture and things with sharp edges out of the way

- remove anything from the mouth and do not attempt to make him drink
- wait quietly with the child until he is aware what has happened and can cope
- ask if he wants to rest before returning to work
- do not ring for an ambulance unless the child has an injury or the seizure has lasted more than 5–10 minutes
- explain to classmates what has happened and how they can help
- help the student to catch up with missed work
- always inform parents of an attack.

◆ Fragile X Syndrome

Fragile X Society

01371 875100
www.fragilex.org.uk

This is the most common inherited learning disability, caused by a defect in the X chromosome. Both males and females act as carriers. The incidence is estimated at 1:3,000, with male sufferers more common and most severely affected. It is thought that many in the population are not diagnosed, as the range of intellectual, emotional and behavioural impairments is considerable.

Characteristics

- Child is 'floppy' with delayed developmental milestones in early years.
- Gross and fine motor co-ordination is poor, affecting writing.
- Frequent speech, language or communication problems with sound articulation and fluency, leading to rapid speech, jargon and repeated phrases and a tendency to digress.
- Possible difficulty with reasoning, and with learning concepts and number processes.
- Often impulsive and disruptive.
- Often unable to settle, with obsessions such as hand-flapping.
- Dislikes busy environments and is easily overwhelmed.
- Upset by smells and noise.
- Over-sensitive to imagined criticism, constantly needing reassurance.
- Requires security and routine.

Management

There is no cure; the key to improvement is the relationships made with significant adults – parents and educators – who can work patiently by promoting change and development.

TIPS:

- ◆ Communicate regularly with the child and parents to minimize problems.
- ◆ Enlist the advice and services of physio and occupational therapists in making classroom adaptations and providing suitable equipment to help gross and fine motor movements.
- ◆ Use adapted keyboards or voice-activated software packages if finger movement is too restricted for completing work.
- ◆ Use a sloping desk and suitable seating to help counter handwriting difficulties, different sizes and shapes of pens, handouts or copies of notes, and a dictaphone for note-taking.
- ◆ Talk about problems with peers in PSHE lessons and enlist their help.
- ◆ Make lesson aims clear and the learning situation uncluttered.
- ◆ Use straightforward language for instructions.
- ◆ Keep to routines and explain changes carefully.
- ◆ Set positive objectives to deal with behaviour and nip bad habits or obsessions in the bud.
- ◆ Use praise for rewarding appropriate behaviour.
- ◆ Keep records to revisit successful strategies.
- ◆ Use a buddy system to help at break times.

Classroom organization

- ◆ Fragile X students have great emotional needs, so provide a key worker to support on a personal level.
- ◆ Give as much personal space as possible, to avoid a feeling of claustrophobia.
- ◆ Set up a structure for communication between school and home.
- ◆ Use therapists to devise suitable movement programmes.
- ◆ Reduce writing demands and use oral as well as written testing methods.
- ◆ Allow work to be word-processed for recording purposes.
- ◆ Plan for transfers.
- ◆ Give constant encouragement and support.
- ◆ Facilitate out-of-school activities, because the child may feel social isolation.

◆ Hearing impairments

The British Association of Teachers of the Deaf

www.batod.org.uk

Hearing impairment is a generic term to describe all types and degrees of hearing loss. The cause is some interruption in the sound pathways from the outer ear to the brain (see diagram below). In the outer ear, which is the visible part, sound waves travel along the external auditory canal and hit the ear drum (tympanic membrane), which lies across the canal, causing it to vibrate. The vibrations transmit through the air-filled middle ear and are greatly amplified by the ossicular chain of three tiny bones. The inner ear is a fluid-filled space containing the cochlea, which turns the mechanical vibrations from the middle ear into nerve impulses activating fibres of the auditory nerve. Sound is then processed and analysed in the central nervous system. The key tasks involved in hearing are:

◆ **detection** (awareness and localization)

◆ **attention** (selecting the sound from its background)

◆ **discrimination** (acoustic and segmental differentiation)

◆ **organization** (differentiating intonation and stress, sequencing, synthesis to achieve overall meaning and retention).

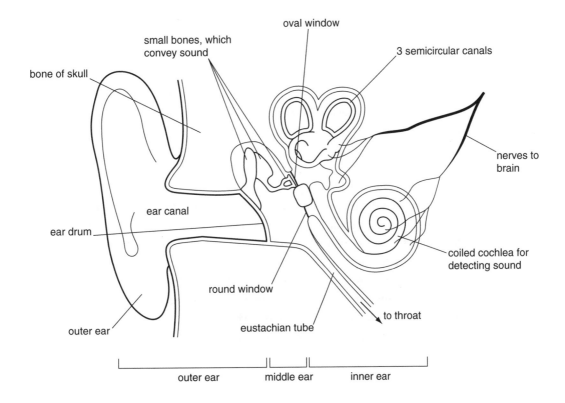

159

General characteristics

◆ Inattention – appearing to hear only when she wants to; daydreams.

◆ Talks more loudly than normal or talks less and is withdrawn.

◆ Turns up sound on TV, audio player or computer.

◆ Says 'Pardon?' or 'What?' frequently.

◆ Fails to hear sound generated out of visual range.

◆ Experiences pain if suffering from glue ear.

◆ Tiredness due to extra attention required.

◆ Tinnitus, vertigo (cochlea is linked to balance organs).

◆ Sensitivity to sound.

◆ Makes inappropriate comments and may be disruptive in lessons.

◆ Confuses words that sound similar ('fat', 'that', 'vat', for example).

◆ Shows limited vocabulary, syntax and sound use, finding it difficult to repeat accurately.

◆ Misinterprets information or responds only to part of it.

◆ Watches others carefully to see what they do, so she can follow.

◆ Suffers frequent colds and coughs.

To understand hearing impairment, it is necessary to appreciate two key features of sound measurement – *level* and *frequency*. Sound level is the volume of sound measured in decibels (dB). At a standard distance of one metre (three feet):

◆ whispered speech = 30 dB

◆ normal speech = 60 dB

◆ loud shouting = 90 dB.

Sound frequency is the main physical basis of our subjective impression of pitch. Frequency determines whether we hear sound as high or low, and is measured in hertz (Hz). The lowest C on the piano is 32 Hz and the highest is 2,000 Hz (2 KHz). The normal hearing range for people is 100–10,000 Hz (10 KHz).

Hearing can be impaired in the range of frequencies one can hear, or in the volume of sound, or both. With regard to frequency – unless a person can hear within the range 500–2,000 Hz (2 KHz), it is likely that speech development will be affected. The diagram on the next page shows an audiogram, which is a graphic representation of hearing. A calibrated machine generates pure tones at different frequencies and intensities, and presents them to one ear at a time through headphones in an 'air conduction' or 'bone conduction' test. A person's ability to hear pure tones, presented at different frequencies and intensities, is plotted on to the audiogram and the curve is compared with the normal minimal audibility curve (which would be a horizontal straight line at a hearing loss of 0 dB). This kind of audiometric test is the most commonly used measure of hearing impairment and provides a visual picture of a person's response to sounds.

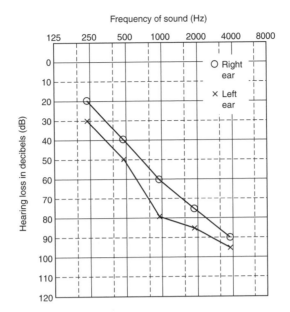

The audiogram above shows the responses of a 13-year-old boy with a high-frequency loss in both ears, being more severe in the left. This type of hearing loss means that lower frequency vowel sounds are heard moderately well, but high frequency consonants cannot be heard, which may be reflected in the person's speech and, therefore, writing. A sample of this boy's free writing is given below.

> There is a dog. The dog name is Borage. The dog got white and brown. The dog got wet nose. The dog is eating the food. The dog got waggy ears. The dog got tail. The dog got four leg.

The description of the dog demonstrates a limited range of syntax and grammatical ability, with sentences having stereotypical openings, which is characteristic of this type of hearing loss.

In younger children, glue ear (otitis media) is a very common problem, resulting in some hearing impairment. It involves fluid collecting in the middle ear and becoming thick and infected, interfering with sound conduction. As many as four out of five children have glue ear before school age, which prevents them from learning speech accurately if it continues.

The table below shows the characteristics of different levels of hearing loss.

Decibel loss (dB)	Impairment
0	none
1–40	slight to mild – some difficulties understanding speech
41–70	moderate – difficulty with normal (41–55) and loud (56–70) speech
71–90	severe – limited understanding of speech
96 plus	profound – rarely showing understanding of speech

Types of loss

- ◆ Mono aural loss affects one ear only and presents no problems in one-to-one talk situations, but in large groups and in big spaces there are difficulties in discriminating and locating sounds, which depends on input from two ears for correct processing.
- ◆ Conductive loss is an impediment in the transmission of sound to the cochlea, caused by a build up of wax, a foreign object or excess middle ear fluid, which becomes thick and infected leading to inflammation (glue ear or otitis media).
- ◆ Sensory loss is caused by nerve damage before or after birth.

Management

Conductive losses may respond to medicines. If the problem is persistent, miniature ventilation tubes (grommets) are inserted into the ear drum, staying in place for 6–12 months and then falling out to allow the small hole to heal. This procedure may need repeating to keep the ear drained and hearing improved.

Sensory losses cannot be restored, but hearing aids may be fitted to make better use of residual hearing by increasing sound volume. Some children are offered cochlear implants, which if successful give the possibility of increased hearing.

TIPS:

- ◆ Those with mild losses need to look directly at the speaker. Ambient noise in the classroom can be dampened down by carpets and curtains, but if this is not possible ask a hearing expert for specific advice about your particular context.
- ◆ Moderate and severe losses need visual clues, such as lip reading and sign language. Radio aids can be used, the transmitter worn by the speaker (teacher) and the receiver by the child.
- ◆ Do not shout, but speak slowly and clearly and use supportive gestures.
- ◆ Remember that children with glue ear usually feel under par and are often listless.

Classroom organization

- ◆ Always attract the child's attention, by calling his name before asking a question or giving an instruction. Step forward out of the crowd to make focus easier.
- ◆ Do not stand with your back to the light, so your face movements are in shadow.
- ◆ Talk face to face, sitting or bending to the same level in a one-to-one exchange.
- ◆ Seat the child in the front of the class, where he can see the teacher clearly.
- ◆ Cut down background noise and provide good lighting.
- ◆ Keep instructions short and simple.

- Present one source of information at a time, because it is difficult for the child to focus on what you are saying as well as looking at a book or watching the writing on a board.
- Explain the problem to classmates and suggest how they can be helpful.
- Sound–symbol work will be a problem in the literacy hour and the child will need the support of a teaching assistant, trained to deal with hearing loss.

◆ Left-handed writers

Anything Left-Handed

020 8770 3722
www.anythingleft-handed.co.uk

We live in a right-handed world, because only 10 per cent of people are left-handed. Parents and teachers used to discourage children from doing things with their left hand, but nowadays they are allowed to develop without pressure. There are different types of preferences. A student may write and draw with the left hand but kick a ball with the right and be left-eye dominant. This is called being 'cross-lateral'; such children tend to be clumsy because their eye and hand do not co-ordinate well.

Management

Writing causes most concerns for left-handers in school; more practice is needed at writing tasks than is needed by right-handers.

Characteristics

- Since the writing pattern is left to right, left-handers push the pen across the page, which is much harder than pulling it.
- As they cannot see what they have written, letter formation tends to be tricky and can be inaccurate.
- Pencil grip is often strange and not the 'tripod' grip adopted by most right-handers.

TIP:
- Choose paper and pens that are easy to use. Do not expect left-handers to cope well with crayons and sugar paper.
- Encourage the student to experiment and find writing materials that are comfortable, encouraging the use of pencil grips in early stages.
- As left-handers cannot use right-handed scissors, ensure left-handed scissors are available in class.

Class organization

◆ Avoid a situation where a left-handed child is seated with a right-handed one on the left, as they will both be fighting for elbow space.

◆ Put together materials for practice at home. Discuss the issue with parents, who might not be aware their child has more difficulties than the norm.

◆ Ensure the child knows how to achieve a good writing posture (see below).

◆ Furniture must be the right size, so both feet can be on the floor and arms are comfortable on the table.

◆ Raising the seat can give a better view of writing.

◆ Sloping writing surfaces often help.

◆ Position of the writing paper is vital; it needs to be tilted to the right for a left-handed writer, as shown in the diagram opposite.

◆ Encourage a relaxed pencil grip (a tripod is easiest). There is no right or wrong about this and when a grip is established it is very difficult to change, so never force the issue. Tight grips force the child to press hard on the paper and twist the hand awkwardly, so writing is uncomfortable and difficult to sustain. See the diagrams below for a relaxed grip position.

◆ Demonstrate letter formation with your left hand for students who are left-handed.

◆ Be aware of extra difficulties in doing practical tasks.

good grip

bad grip

left-hander | right-hander   left-hander | right-hander

◆ Moderate learning difficulties (MLD)

Foundation for People with Learning Disabilities

020 7802 0300
www.learningdisabilities.org.uk

This is the largest group of children and young people with special educational needs. They are sometimes referred to as having global learning difficulties (GLD) and are increasingly found in mainstream schools. In the past, these students were known as slow learners or remedials, and are generally found in the bottom sets in classes. School is not easy for them, and self-esteem is often low, especially in secondary school. As a result, behaviour is often unacceptable, as they look for a way of avoiding failure by showing bravado to impress peers.

Characteristics

- ◆ Difficulties with receptive and expressive language in speech and writing.
- ◆ Limited understanding of abstract concepts, leading to problems dealing with mathematics.
- ◆ Immature emotional and social development.
- ◆ Short attention span.
- ◆ Under-developed co-ordination skills affecting gross and fine motor performance.
- ◆ Lack of critical (logical) and creative (lateral) thinking.
- ◆ Inability to generalize learning in new contexts.

165

Children with MLD have associated difficulties in the areas of general comprehension, auditory and visual short- and long-term memory, sequencing skills, dyspraxia (lack of co-ordination), general organization, speech, language and communication. A variety of syndromes and medical conditions are found among this group.

TIPS:

- Build self-esteem, finding ways to make the MLD student shine, as he lags behind peers in most areas of performance.
- Find out details about the child and use assessment data to discover strengths and weaknesses.
- Observe how the child responds to different learning and communication styles.
- Make learning objectives realistic for all lessons, so success is possible.
- Give extra time to finish tasks.
- Check understanding constantly.
- Establish supportive relationships.
- Use praise continually and keep morale boosted.
- Liaise with the SENCO for advice about resources: ICT software, language master, word banks, differentiated texts and writing frames.

Classroom management

- Establish clear rules, routines and responsibilities, so the student knows what is expected of him.
- Establish what the child knows and start from the point where he is on firm ground.
- Keep tasks very short and build variety into them.
- Short, daily practice of multiplication tables, telling the time and new vocabulary is more effective than one long session.
- 'Show and tell' is a more effective strategy than just talking about something.
- Provide concrete examples of subject content and make lessons participatory.
- Provide a teaching assistant who is available to clarify and support.
- Repeat information regularly and in different ways.

◆ Muscular dystrophy (MD)

The Muscular Dystrophy Campaign

020 7720 8055

www.muscular-dystrophy.org

This general term describes a group of around 20 genetic disorders that involve progressive muscle weakness. Duchenne's muscular dystrophy is the most common childhood form affecting only males, but other types involve both sexes. Becker muscular dystrophy is a rare, mild form only affecting males; it progresses slowly with a few signs in early childhood, such as late walking, slow running and cramps. Problems become more apparent in teenagers, who will be slow walkers and have difficulties with stairs. Most people with this latter type have a reasonable lifespan and generally cope well in school, other than in sport, with few associated learning problems.

The conditions are caused by a fault on a particular gene that results in damaged muscle fibres. Some individuals remain stable, while others degenerate rapidly and life expectancy varies a great deal. The inheritance pattern is known as autosomal recessive, meaning both parents are carriers and have a one-in-four chance of passing on the condition. The incidence is about 1:50,000.

Types and characteristics

1 **Dystrophy** – weakness affecting all muscles.

2 **Dystrophy + learning difficulties** – general or specific.

3 **Dystrophy + eye abnormalities + learning difficulties** – general or specific.

◆ Floppiness (hypotonia).

◆ Limited head control.

◆ Delayed motor milestones such as crawling and walking.

◆ Tightness in joints: hands, wrists, elbows, ankles, knees, hips.

◆ Tendency to hip dislocation.

Management

There is no cure for this distressing condition, but there are ways to alleviate symptoms. Physio, occupational and speech and language therapists will be able to advise the school on suitable handling. A child with MD can remain fairly stable but if the condition progresses rapidly, respiratory failure is possible. Some children learn to walk with callipers commonly used to provide support for weak muscles. Most children, however, will have to rely on a wheelchair for mobility.

◆ **167**

TIPS:

- Communicate with child and parents regularly to keep abreast of current needs.
- Do not assume that developments will or will not take place. Work with the individual and other professionals involved, for best results.
- Seek advice from therapists on suitable adaptations and useful equipment.
- Ensure positive attitudes from peers through PSHE.
- Avoid isolation and encourage after-school activities.
- Make use of computers and computer aids to help communication, if appropriate.
- Plan ahead, taking into account the varying pace of deterioration.
- Build self-esteem and encourage interests.

Classroom organization

- Think about classroom layout, use of stairs and so on, as access is about getting around spaces as well as getting into them.
- Ensure the student has opportunities for regular exercise, especially swimming, as it helps maintain muscle tone.
- Incorporate choice, which is important for self-esteem and control.
- Facilitate counselling for staff and students, as dealing with a progressive disorder can precipitate strong emotions and be very distressing for all concerned.
- Muscle weakness can make daily living very tough, so a warm, accepting, friendly, positive atmosphere is vital, to provide the base for the child to feel she can cope and succeed.

◆ Tourette's syndrome (TS)

Tourette Syndrome (UK) Association

0845 458 1252

www.tsa.org.uk

This is one of a number of tic disorders, characterized by involuntary rapid or sudden movement or sound that is constantly repeated. It can be triggered by infection, but it is antibodies that do this. The cause is an inability to regulate a neuro-transmitter called dopamine, which results in impaired action of various nerve cell receptor sites. This neurobiological disorder is genetically inherited. It is estimated that 3 per cent of the population suffer, with a ratio of 4:1 males to females. Children follow the normal distribution curve regarding intelligence, but are likely to have more learning problems.

Types and characteristics

◆ Pure Tourette's syndrome (TS) is often undiagnosed with no other associated conditions.

◆ Full-blown TS includes extremes such as coprolalia (repetition of obscene words) and/or coproproxia (repetition of obscene gestures).

◆ 'TS plus' is where associated conditions are present, such as attention deficit hyperactivity disorder, obsessive compulsive disorder, oppositional defiant disorder, self-injurious behaviour, aggression, depression, gross/fine motor problems, organizational difficulties and reading comprehension difficulties.

◆ Echolalia – repetition of what was last heard.

◆ Echopraxia – imitation of actions last seen.

◆ Tics tend to disappear in sleep, but not always and are worse at stressful times.

◆ Tics may subside when the child is in a period of extreme concentration.

◆ If people suppress tics, they return with a vengeance when the person relaxes.

◆ One in five TS children have transient tics, which last a few weeks or months.

◆ Chronic tics remain unchanged and a person may have several types.

Management

Medication may be necessary and depends on the severity. The sufferer needs support for the condition, as it is often not understood how it affects the individual child.

TIPS:

◆ Talk to the child and parents and decide how to help most effectively.

◆ Prevent teasing from others.

◆ Allow extra time for tasks to avoid stress.

◆ Provide 'time out' if the tic is disruptive.

◆ Have a sign, so the child can leave class to relieve tics privately.

◆ Encourage the student to self-monitor, so he realizes when he needs a break.

◆ Allow him to sit at the back to avoid staring from peers.

◆ Provide a separate room for exams.

◆ Watch for depression.

◆ Never punish a tic.

Classroom organization

◆ Make sure all staff and peers understand the problems.

◆ Allow flexibility – for example, if reading is affected by eye or neck tics, provide an alternative.

◆ Use multisensory strategies in tasks.

◆ Pair with a mentor if tics make an activity unsafe.

◆ If the tic is a touching one, allow for a 'buffer zone' of space around the child.

- ◆ Plan carefully for exciting or stressful occasions.
- ◆ Provide a library or quiet area for work.
- ◆ Break work into small chunks as tics are exhausting.
- ◆ Use a computer to cut down on handwriting.
- ◆ Seek positive attitudes from peers through PSHE.
- ◆ Avoid isolation and encourage after-school activities.
- ◆ Make use of computers and computer aids to help communication, if appropriate.
- ◆ Plan ahead, taking into account the varying pace of deterioration.
- ◆ Build self-esteem and encourage interests.

◆ Visual impairment

Royal National Institute for the Blind

0845 766 9999

www.rnib.org.uk

The majority of children with sight problems are educated in mainstream schools where, given appropriate support, they usually do well. In some cases, however, difficulties are not detected or understood and these cause problems. Incidence is 4:10,000 among children.

Types and characteristics

- ◆ **Visual acuity** is measured by the Snellen and Jaeger charts. The Snellen chart comprises lines of letters in progressively smaller typeface. The size of the letters on each line is designed so that it is known at what distance a person with normal acuity can read that line accurately. It is represented as:

  visual acuity = distance from the chart ÷ letter size

  If a child has visual acuity of 6:36, it means she can read letters at 6 metres that someone with normal acuity could read at 36 metres. This ratio is a guide to the level at which a child will need vision aids and can be registered blind. The Jaeger chart assesses near vision, using lines of print of different sizes, and gives an indication of suitable reading material – normal print, large print books and so on.

- ◆ **Fields of vision** define limitations in the area that a person can see. When looking directly forward with one eye at a time, the object in the focus of vision is seen most clearly, whereas those around are less clear. The range of what is seen without moving the eye is the field of vision.

- ◆ **Colour vision**, if defective, affects education where colour is used in teaching. 1:50 are affected, mostly males, with difficulties between reds and greens most common. The Ishihara Test of colour vision comprises cards with numbers or patterns in spots of contrasting colours. The patterns, which can be seen, differ according to degree of normal colour vision.

◆ **Associated conditions** include malformations of the cornea, lens or globe of the eye; retinitis pigmentosa (hereditary degenerative disease of the retina); effects of maternal rubella; Usher's syndrome (genetic condition causing progressive visual impairment); and sensori-neural loss. About 35 per cent of children with severe or profound hearing loss also have visual impairments.

◆ **Range of impairments** covers minor impairment through to blindness.

Characteristics

◆ Inflamed, weepy, cloudy or bloodshot eyes.

◆ Squints, eyes not aligned and working together.

◆ Rapid, involuntary eye movements, blinking, rubbing or screwing up of eyes.

◆ Discomfort in bright light.

◆ Head held at an awkward angle or book at an unusual angle or distance.

◆ Headaches or dizziness

◆ Clumsiness, missing the table when putting things on it, bumping into objects.

◆ Failure to respond to questions, commands or gestures, unless addressed by name.

Management

Some problems such as squints, which are the result of muscle imbalance, can be corrected with surgery. Acuity problems are corrected with prescriptive glasses. Otherwise, difficulties have to be managed by using a range of visual aids. It is even possible to have 'readers' that will scan written material and convert it into computer-generated speech. While assessments of visual acuity, field of vision and colour vision are important, an assessment of functional vision is essential to determine a student's educational needs.

When it is thought that vision is impaired, educational advice must be sought from a qualified teacher of the blind according to regulations (1983) following the 1981 Education Act. Support is necessary for student and teachers and includes:

◆ planned contact with visual impairment advisory service to discuss issues and receive advice

◆ curriculum advice on relevant teaching materials

◆ advice on low vision aids and equipment

◆ advice on requisite illuminations

◆ opportunities for students to get to know the school and its layout.

TIPS:

- ◆ Encourage wearing of glasses, if recommended, and check them for cleanliness.
- ◆ Use the Visually Impaired specialist teacher to advise on the condition and its implications.
- ◆ Give clear instructions and descriptions, as gestures and facial expressions are often misread.
- ◆ Use the child's name to get attention.
- ◆ Sit the child at the front and near to the board, television or OHP.
- ◆ Allow extra time for finishing tasks.

Classroom organization

- ◆ Provide the child with his own resource materials, so that he does not have to share.
- ◆ Do not stand near a window that will silhouette you while talking with the class.
- ◆ Make sure work areas are well lit with no glare. Some visually impaired children are photophobic (sensitive to light) and more comfortable in shade.
- ◆ Present short tasks to prevent tiring.
- ◆ Draw attention to wall displays, as they may not be noticed.
- ◆ Encourage tidiness and identification of personal space. The child's peg or locker should be at the end of a row to be found more easily.
- ◆ Find out about useful equipment, such as talking scales.
- ◆ Enlarge the type size in 'in-house' resource sheets to 16 or 18 point, using good spacing for information. Avoid italics and use lower case, because ascenders and descenders give more distinctive shape. Use short lines of text and unjustified margins with paper that is matt rather than glossy. Avoid clutter and use strong contrasts to highlight important things.

Appendix 5

Organizing learning: a brief history

◆ Elementary education

Systems of education evolved from the transformations of society that took place in the eighteenth and nineteenth centuries (Mann, 1979). Formally, education had been only for the rich, privileged sectors of the population. With the springing up of large factories and the move from rural to urban communities, schools for the poor became common. Children were drilled in a curriculum mainly concerned with teaching values, virtues, literacy, numeracy, hygiene, physical maintenance, domestic skills and basic knowledge about the world. Pioneers viewed education as the instrument of moral transformation necessary to survive new urban communities. The first schools were for primary aged children. Secondary education only emerged after 1904, when new forms of transport were opening up possibilities in an increasingly mechanized and technological world demanding new knowledge and skills.

◆ The tripartite system

The end of the First World War signalled a shift in educational philosophy. The Norwood Report (Board of Education, 1943) stated three aims:

1 knowledge for its own sake

2 occupational knowledge and skills for industry, trade and commerce

3 practical studies to balance mind and body: humanities, sciences and arts (including sport).

The Educational Act 1944 was a defining moment in the history of education in the UK, as it bestowed a right for all students to a secondary education based on ability and aptitude, but with ordinary and advanced General Certificates in Education (GCEs) offered only to bright students, in:

◆ grammar schools, with selection at eleven-plus, for the academically able

◆ technical schools for the practically able to pursue careers such as engineering

◆ secondary modern schools for those not fitting the above categories, providing a general education for mainly unskilled workers.

◆ Comprehensive system

Criticisms about parity of esteem and of the increasingly discredited selection procedures began to emerge (Young, 1998). The move towards the comprehensive school was designed to heal the divisions. Schools were to take *all* students within a geographical area and offer choice and diversity in the curriculum. There were different ways of organizing teaching, with setting, streaming and mixed ability classes (from 1970s). The GCE qualifications were supplemented by the Certificate of Secondary Education (CSE), offering a more practical, flexible, new type of examination process that incorporated some of the transferable (key) skills demanded by workplaces.

◆ The national curriculum: The Education Reform Act 1988

The Education Reform Act 1988 changed the nature of the curriculum and its authority. Previously, each school decided what it taught, which resulted in diverse standards across the country. The law now prescribed a consistent set of national standards. The national curriculum was frequently modified in its early years but current ministerial orders have been in place since 1995.

There are three core subjects (English, mathematics, science) and the rest are called foundation subjects (information technology, design and technology, history, geography, music, art, physical education, a modern foreign language and – from 2002 – citizenship). Specific requirements concerning these subjects vary according to student ages. Teaching and assessment is divided into four key stages:

- ◆ Key Stage 1 – up to age 7 (years 1 and 2)
- ◆ Key Stage 2 – up to age 11 (years 3–6)
- ◆ Key Stage 3 – up to age 14 (years 7–9)
- ◆ Key Stage 4 – up to age 16 (years 10–11).

At Key Stages 1 and 2, English, mathematics and science have to be taught according to detailed programmes of study. Information technology, design and technology, history, geography, music, art and physical education must be taught, but after 1999 schools have been given more freedom in their approach. Since September 1998, however, schools have been required to devote an hour per day to literacy, and since 1999 a similar time to numeracy. There is no modern language requirement at these stages. We might question this decision in light of our global economy and need for multilingual skills.

At Key Stage 3, a modern foreign language is included in the requirements and subjects are taught according to detailed programmes in the national curriculum documents. At Key Stage 4, history, geography, music and art are no longer compulsory. At a time when individuals are beginning to think about their place in the world and how they can contribute to it creatively, they may find that they are no longer able to include the relevant subjects to help them.

The national curriculum is not intended to take up all the time in school and there are no statutory requirements as to how schools programme their activities. The Dearing report (1994) made recommendations indicating that, at Key Stages 3 and 4, English should occupy 14 per cent of school time; science 13 per cent; mathematics 12 per cent; technology, foreign languages, religious education and physical education each 5 per cent, and the remaining 43 per cent should be discretionary with a balance of other specified subjects.

National curriculum Standard Assessment Tests (SATs)

The national curriculum is shaped by its assessment procedures. Gipps and Stobart (1993) have described these as the 'assessment tail wagging the curriculum dog'! The framework was established as a result of the work of the Task Group on Assessment and Testing, chaired by Paul Black (DES, 1989). It represented a major break with past tradition and ownership, by establishing national, externally marked tests at ages 7, 11 and 14, known as the Standard Assessment Tests (SATs). The programmes of study for each subject are published in booklets (and online) by both English and Welsh education departments. Each subject divides into different attainment targets. Those for the core subjects are shown below.

Attainment targets for national curriculum core subjects		
English	**Mathematics**	**Science**
Speaking and listening	Using and applying mathematics	Experimental and investigative science
Reading	Number	Life processes and living things
Writing	Shape, space, measures and handling data (KS 2–4)	Materials and their properties
	Algebra (KS 3–4)	Physical processes

References

◆ Chapter One

Ainscow, M. (1995) 'Education for all: making it happen', *Support for Learning* 10(4): 147–54

Avramadis, E. and Bayliss, P. (1998) 'An enquiry into children with emotional and behaviour difficulties in two schools in the south west of England', *Emotional and Behaviour Difficulties* 3(3): 25–35

Beresford, B. (1995) *Expert Opinions: A National Survey of Parents Caring for a Severely Disabled Child* (Bristol: The Policy Press)

Booth, T., Ainscow, M., Black-Hawkins, K., Vaughn, M. and Shaw, L. (2000) *Index for Inclusion: Developing Learning and Participation in Schools* (Bristol: CSIE)

Bourne, J., Bridges, L. and Searle, C. (1995) *Outcast England: How Schools Exclude Black Children* (London: Institute of Race Relations)

Cooper, P. (2001) *We Can Work It Out – a review of what works with SEBD* (Barnados)

Cunningham, C. and Davis, H. (1985) *Working with Parents: Frameworks for Collaboration* (Milton Keynes: Open University Press)

Department for Education (DfE) (1993) *Schools Requiring Special Measures* (Circular 17/93) (London: HMSO)

Department for Education and Employment/Qualifications and Curriculum Authority (DfEE/QCA) (1999) *The National Curriculum Handbook for Primary Teachers in England* (London: DfEE/QCA)

Department for Education and Employment (DfEE) (2000) *SEN Code of Practice on the Identification and Assessment of Students with Special Educational Needs* and *SEN Thresholds: Good Practice Guidelines on Identification and Provision for Students with Special Educational Needs* (London: DfEE)

Department for Education and Science (DES) (1989) *The Education Reform Act 1988: The School Curriculum and Assessment* (Circular 5/89) (London: DES)

Department for Education and Skills (DfES) (2001) *Special Educational Needs Code of Practice* (London: DfES)

Ferri, E. and Smith, K. (1996) *Parenting in the 1990s* (London: Family Policy Studies Centre in association with the Joseph Rowntree Foundations)

Frederickson, N. and Cline, T. (eds) (1995) *Assessing the Learning Environments of Children with Special Educational Needs* (London: Educational Psychology Publishing)

Goacher, B., Evans, J., Welton, J. and Wedell, K. (1988) *Policy and Provision for Special Educational Needs* (London: Cassell)

Hammersley, M. (1997) 'Educational research and teaching: a response to David Hargreaves' TTA lecture', *British Educational Research Journal* 23(2): 141–61 (a Taylor and Francis Ltd journal – see www.tandf.co.uk/journals/titles/09540261.html)

Haskey, J. (1996) 'The proportion of married couples who divorce: past patterns and present prospects', *Population Trends* 83: 25–36

Herrnstein, R.J. (1973) *IQ in the Meritocracy* (Boston: Atlantic Monthly Press)

Hillage, J., Pearson, R., Anderson, A. and Tamkin, P. (1998) *Excellence in Research on Schools* (research report RR74) (Suffolk: DfEE Publications) 60

Hornby, G. (1995) *Working with Parents of Children with Special Needs* (London: Cassell) 20–1

Inner London Education Authority (ILEA) (1984) *Survey of Characteristics of Students in Inner London Schools* (London: Inner London Education Authority) 15

Jelly, M., Fuller, A. and Byars, R. (2000) *Involving Students in Practice* (London: David Fulton)

Kelley-Laine, K. (1998) 'Parents as partners in schooling: the current state of affairs', *Childhood Education* 74(6): 342–5

Masters, J.M. and Furman, W. (1981) 'Popularity, individual friendship selection and specific peer interaction among children', *Developmental Psychology* 17: 344–50

McKee, W.T. and Witt, J.C. (1990) 'Effective teaching: a review of instructional and environmental variables', in Gutkin, T.B. and Reynolds, C.R. (eds) *The Handbook of School Psychology* (New York: Wiley)

O'Donnell, K. (1999) 'Lesbian and gay families: legal perspectives', in Jagger, G. and Wright, C. (eds) *Changing Family Value* (London: Routledge)

Office for National Statistics (2003) *The Annual Abstract of Statistics in Britain* (London: HMSO)

Peach, C. (1982) 'The growth and distribution of the black population in Britain 1945–1980', in Coleman, D.A. (ed) *Demography of Immigrants and Minority Groups in the United Kingdom* (London: Academic Press)

Rehal, A. (1989) 'Involving Asian parents in the statementing procedure – the way forward', *Educational Psychology in Practice*, 4(4): 189–97

Riddell, S. (1996) 'Gender and special educational needs', in Lloyd, G. (ed) *'Knitting Progress Unsatisfactory': Gender and Special Issues in Education* (Edinburgh: Moray House Publications)

Robson, A. (1989) 'Special needs and special educational needs', Paper, Inner London Education Authority

Ruddock, J. and Flutter, J. (2000) 'Students' participation and student perspective: carving a new order of experience', *Cambridge Journal of Education* 30(1): 75–90

Sage, R. (2000a) *The Communication Opportunity Group Scheme* (COGS) (Leicester: The University of Leicester)

Sage, R. (2000b) *Class Talk* (Stafford: Network Educational Press)

Thomas, G. (1992) *Effective Classroom Teamwork: Support or Intrusion?* (London: Routledge)

Thomas, R.M. (1994) 'The meaning and significance of *ethnicity* in educational discourse', *International Review of Education* 40(1): 74–80

Tomlinson, S. (1984) 'Minority groups in English conurbations', in Williams, P. (ed) *Special Education in Minority Communities* (Milton Keynes: Open University Press) 21–2

Tomlinson, S. (2000) 'Ethnic minorities and education: new disadvantages', in Cox, T. (ed) *Combating Educational Disadvantage: Meeting the Needs of Vulnerable Children* (London: Falmer Press) 28

Upton, G. (1990) 'The Education Reform Act and special educational needs', *Newsletter of the Association for Child Psychology and Psychiatry* 12(5): 3–8

◆ Chapter Two

Anderson, J.A. (1995) 'Towards a framework for matching teaching and learning styles for diverse populations', in Sims, R.K. and Sims, S.J. (eds) *The Importance of Learning Styles: Understanding the Implications for Learning Course Design and Education* (London: Greenwood Press)

Atkinson, J.W. (1974) 'The mainstream of achievement-oriented activity', in Atkinson, J.W. and Rayner, J.O. (eds) *Motivation and Achievement* (New York: Halstead) 13–41

Bell, N. (1991) *Visualizing and Verbalizing* (Paso Robles, California: Academy of Reading Publications)

Bloom, B.S. (1956) *Taxonomy of Educational Objectives: cognitive domain* (New York: David McKay)

Boxall, M. (1996) 'The nurture group in the primary school', in Bennathan, M. and Boxall, M. (eds) *Effective Intervention in Primary Schools: Nurture Groups* (London: David Fulton) 18–38

Burt, C. (1957) *The Causes and Treatment of Backwardness*, 4th edn (London: King and Son)

Cameron, R.J. and Reynolds, A.R. (1999) 'Learning style and metacognition', in Frederickson, N.J. and Cameron, R.J. (eds) *Psychology in Education Portfolio* (Windsor: NFER-Nelson)

Cartledge, G. and Milburn, J.F. (1996) *Cultural Diversity and Social Skills Instruction: understanding ethnic and gender differences* (Champaign, IL: Research Press)

Ceci, S.J. (1996) *On Intelligence* (Cambridge, MA: Cambridge University Press)

Deci, E.L. and Ryan, R.M. (1985) *Intrinsic Motivation and Self-Determination in Human Behaviour* (New York: Plenum)

Erwin, P.G. (1994) 'Effectiveness of social skills training: a meta-analytic study', *Counselling Psychology Quarterly* 7(3): 305–10

Eysenck, H.J. and Eysenck, S.B.G. (1975) *Manual of the Eysenck Personality Questionnaire* (London: Hodder and Stoughton)

Feuerstein, R. (1979) *The Dynamic Assessment of Retarded Performers: The Learning Potential Assessment Device* (Baltimore, MD: University Park Press) 8

Foster, S.L., Martines, C.R. and Kulberg, A.M. (1996) 'Race, ethnicity and children's peer relations', in Ollrndick, T.H. and Prinz, R.J. (eds) *Advances in Clinical Child Psychology* No. 18 (New York: Plenum Press)

Frederickson, N. and Graham, B. (1999) 'Social skills and emotional intelligence', in Frederickson, N. and Cameron, R.J. (eds) *Psychology in Education Portfolio* (Windsor: NFER-Nelson)

Furnham, A. and Argyle, A. (1981) 'The theory, practice and application of social skills training', *International Journal of Behavioural Social Work* 1: 125–43

Gardner, H. (1993a) *Frames of Mind: The theory of multiple intelligences*, 2nd edn (London: Fontana Press) xiv

Gardner, H. (1993b) *The Unschooled Mind* (London: Fontana Press)

Goleman, D. (1996) *Emotional Intelligence* (London: Bloomsbury)

Greenberg, M.T., Kusche, C.A., Cook, E.T. and Quamma, J.P. (1995) 'Promoting emotional competence in school aged children: the effects of the PATHS curriculum', *Development and Psychopathology* 7: 117–36

Hickson, J., Land, A.J. and Aikman, G. (1994) 'Learning style differences in middle school students from four different ethnic backgrounds', *School Psychology International* 15(4): 349–59

Jenson, A.R. (1969) 'How much can we boost IQ and scholastic achievement?', *Harvard Educational Review* 39: 1–123

Male, D. (1996) 'Who goes to MLD schools?', *British Journal of Special Education* 23(1): 35–41

Masters, J.M. and Furman, W. (1981) 'Popularity, individual friendship selection and specific peer interaction among children', *Developmental Psychology* 17: 344–50

McCarthy, J.J .and Kirk, S.A. (1961) *The Illinois Test of Psycholinguistic Abilities* (Urbana: University of Illinois Press)

McKenna, P. (1990) 'Learning implications of field dependence-independence: cognitive style versus cognitive ability', *Applied Cognitive Psychology* 4: 425–37

Miller, L. (1984) 'Problem solving hypothesis testing and language disorders', in Wallach, G.P. and Butler, K.G. (eds), *Language Learning Disabilities in School-Age Children* (Baltimore, Maryland: Williams and Wilkins)

Mobilia, W., Fox, P., Monether, P. and Gordon, R. (2001) *Education by Design: Critical Skills: Level 1 and Level 2* (Stafford: Network Educational Press)

Moreno, J.L. (1934) *Who Shall Survive?* (Washington: Nervous and Mental Disease Publishing Company)

Mosley, J. (1996) *Quality Circle Time* (Wisbech: LDA)

Nicholls, C.W. (1991) *Manual: Assessment of Core Goals* (Palo Alto, CA: Consulting Psychologists Press)

Piaget, J. (1964) 'Development and learning', in Ripple, R. and Rockcastle, V. (eds), *Piaget Rediscovered* (Ithaca, NY: Cornell University Press) 7–19

Riding, R.J. and Rayner, S. (1998) *Cognitive Styles and Learning Strategies* (London: David Fulton)

Sage, R. (2000a) *The Communication Opportunity Group Scheme* (COGS) (Leicester: The University of Leicester)

Sage, R. (2000b) *Class Talk* (Stafford: Network Educational Press)

Sage, R. (2003) *Lend Us Your Ears* (Stafford: Network Educational Press)

Salovey, P. and Mayer, J.D. (1990) 'Emotional Intelligence', *Imagination, Cognition and Personality* 9: 185–211

Salovey, P. and Sluyter, D.J. (1997) *Emotional Development and Emotional Intelligence* (New York: Basic Books) 10

Simpson, M. (1997) 'Developing differentiation practices: meeting the needs of students and teachers', *The Curriculum Journal* 8 (1): 85–104

Smith, A. (1998) *Accelerated Learning in Practice* (Stafford: Network Educational Press)

Sternberg, R.J. (1985) *Beyond IQ: A triarchic theory of human intelligence* (Cambridge: Cambridge University Press)

Terman, L.M. (1925) *Genetic Studies of Genius*, Vol. 1 (Stanford, CA: Stanford University Press)

Wechsler, D. (1944) *The Management and Appraisal of Adult Intelligence* (Baltimore, MD: Williams and Wilkins)

Wentzel, K.R. (1991) 'Relations between social competence and academic achievement in early adolescence', *Child Development* 62: 1066–78

◆ Chapter Three

Abreu, G. de (1995) 'Understanding how children experience the relationship between home and school mathematics', *Mind, Culture and Activity: an international journal* 2(2): 119–42

Artiles, A.J., Trent, S.C. and Kuan, L. (1997) 'Learning disabilities empirical research on ethnic minority students: an analysis of 22 years of studies published in selected refereed journals', *Learning Disabilities Research and Practice* 12(2): 82–91

Bee, H. (2000) *The Developing Child*, 9th edn (London: Allyn and Bacon)

Beresford, B. (1995) *Expert Opinions: A National Survey of Parents Caring for a Severely Disabled Child* (Bristol: The Policy Press)

Bourne, J., Bridges, L. and Searle, C. (1995) *Outcast England: How Schools Exclude Black Children* (London: Institute of Race Relations)

Brodie, I. and Berridge, D. (1996) *School Exclusion: Research Themes and Issues* (Luton: University of Luton Press)

Caesar, G., Parchment, M. and Berridge, D. (1994) *Black Perspectives on Services for Children in Need* (London: Barnardo's/National Children's Bureau)

Chau, K.L. (1989) 'Sociocultural dissonance among ethnic minority populations', *Social Casework: The Journal of Contemporary Social Work* 224–30

Cline, T. (1997) 'Special educational needs and language proficiency', in Leung, C. and Cable, C. (eds) *English as an Additional Language: Changing Perspectives* (Watford: National Association for Language Development in the Curriculum) 53–64

Cline, T. and Reason, R. (1993) 'Specific learning difficulties (dyslexia): equal opportunities issues', *British Journal of Special Education* 20(1): 30–4

Coard, B. (1971) *How the West Indian Child is made Educationally Subnormal in the British School System* (London: New Beacon Books)

Cohen, O.P., Fischgrund, M.A. and Redding, R. (1990) 'Deaf children from ethnic, linguistic and racial minority backgrounds: an overview', *American Annals for the Deaf* 135: 67–73

Cohn, T. (1987) 'Sticks and stones may break my bones but names will never hurt me', *Multicultural Teaching* 5(3): 8–11

Condry, J. and Condry, S. (1976) 'Sex differences: a study of the eye of the beholder', *Child Development* 47: 812–19

Condry, J. and Ross, D.F. (1985) 'Sex and aggression: the influence of gender label on the perception of aggression in children', *Child Development* 56: 225–33

Cooper, P., Smith, C.J. and Upton, G. (1994) *Emotional and Behavioural Difficulties: Theory to practice* (London: Routledge)

Cortes, J.B. and Gatti, F.M. (1965) 'Physique and self description of temperament', *Journal of Consulting Psychology* 20: 432–9

Croll, P. and Moses, D. (1985) *One in Five: The Assessment and Incidence of Special Educational Needs* (London: Routledge and Kegan Paul)

Crutchley, A., Conti-Ramsden, G. and Botting, N. (1997) 'Bi-lingual children with specific language impairment and standardised assessments: preliminary findings from a study of children in language units', *International Journal of Bilingualism* 1(2): 117–34

Cummins, J. (1986) 'Empowering minority students: a framework for intervention', *Harvard Educational Review* 56(1): 18–36

Cummins, J. (1989) 'A theoretical framework for bilingual special education', *Exceptional Children* 56(2): 111–119

Department for Education and Employment (DfEE) (1997) Green Paper: *Excellence for All Children* (London: DfEE)

Department for Education and Employment/Qualifications and Curriculum Authority (DfEE/QCA) (1999) *The National Curriculum Handbook for Primary Teachers in England* (London: DfEE) Table E

Department for Education and Science (DES) (1988) Mathematics for Ages 5–16: *Proposals for the National Curriculum* (London: HMSO) paragraphs 10.18–23

Donald, D. (1994) 'Children with special educational needs: the reproduction of disadvantage in poorly served communities', in Dawes, A. and Donald, D. (eds) *Childhood and Adversity: Psychological Perspectives from South African Research* (Claremount, SA: David Philip (Publishing))

Foster S.L., Martinez, C.R. and Kulberg, A.M. (1996) 'Race, ethnicity and children's peer relations', in Ollendick, T.H. and Prinz, R.J. (eds) *Advances in Clinical Child Psychology No. 18* (New York: Plenum Press)

Frederickson, N. and Cline, T. (2002) *Special Educational Needs, Inclusion and Diversity* (Buckingham: Open University Press) 16

Gadhok, K. (1994) 'Languages for intervention', in Martin, D. (ed) *Services to Bilingual Children with Speech and Language Difficulties: Proceedings of the 25th Anniversary AFASIC Conference,* Birmingham, 1993 (London: AFASIC)

Gillborn, D. and Gipps, C. (1996) *Recent Research on the Achievements of Ethnic Minority Students* (London: HMSO)

Gipps, C. and Murphy, P. (1994) *A Fair Test? Assessment, Achievement and Equity* (Buckingham: Open University Press)

Graf, V.L. (1992) 'Minimising the inappropriate referral and placement referral and placement of ethnic minority students in special education', in Cline, T. (ed) *The Assessment of Special Educational Needs: International Perspectives* (London: Routledge) 196

Hanna, G. (1986) 'Sex differences in mathematics achievement of eighth graders in Ontario', *Journal for Research in Mathematics Education* 17: 231–7

Hayden, C. (1997) *Exclusions from Primary Schools* (Buckingham: Open University Press)

Hill, J. (1994) 'The paradox of gender: sex-stereotyping within the statementing procedure', *British Education Research Journal* 20(3): 345–57

Hislam, J. (2002) *Teaching Grammar in the Key Stage 2 Classroom: Case Studies of Trainee Teachers' Subject Knowledge and Application*, Paper to the British Educational Research Association, University of Exeter, September 2002

Holt, J.A. and Allen, T.E. (1989) 'The effects of schools and their curricula on the reading and mathematics achievement of hearing impaired students', *International Journal of Educational Research* 13: 547–62

Huss-Keeler, R.L. (1997) 'Teacher perception of ethnic and linguistic minority parental involvement and its relationship to children's language and literacy learning: a case study', *Teaching and Teacher Education* 13(2): 171–82

Inner London Education Authority (ILEA) (1983) *A Policy for Equality: Race* (London: Inner London Education Authority)

Inner London Education Authority (ILEA) (1990) *SMILE Mathematics* (London: SMILE Centre)

Joseph, G.G. (1993) 'A rationale for a multicultural approach to mathematics', in Nelson, D., Joseph, G.G. and Williams, J. (eds) *Multicultural Mathematics* (Oxford: Oxford University Press) 20–3

Keller, H.R. (1988) 'Children's adaptive behaviour: measure and source generalisability', *Journal of Psychoeducational Assessment* 6: 371–89

Keogh, B.K., Gallimore, R. and Weisner, T. (1997) 'A sociocultural perspective on learning and learning disabilities', *Learning Disabilities Research and Practice* 12(2): 107–13.b

Lawton, D. (1999) *Beyond the National Curriculum* (London: Hodder and Stoughton)

Linn, M.C., Benedictis, T.D., Delucci, K., Harris, A. and Stage, E. (1987) 'Gender differences in National Assessment of Educational Progress science items: what does 'I don't know' really mean?', *Journal of Research in Science Teaching* 24: 267–78

Macpherson Committee of Enquiry (1999) *Report of the Stephen Lawrence Enquiry* (London: HMSO) paragraph 6.34

Madhani, N. (1994) 'Working with speech and language impaired children from linguistic minority communities', in Martin, D. (ed) *Services to Bilingual Children with Speech and Language Difficulties: Proceedings of the 25th Anniversary AFASIC Conference, Birmingham, 1993* (London: AFASIC) 52–9

Martin, D. (2000) 'Communication difficulties in a multicultural context', in Law, J., Parkinson, S. and Tamhe, R. (eds) *Communication Difficulties in Childhood: a practical guide* (Abingdon: Radcliffe Medical Press)

Meherali, R. (1994) 'Being black and deaf', in Laurenzi, C. and Hindley, P. (eds) *Keep Deaf Children in Mind: current issues in mental health* (Leeds: NDCS Family Services)

Molteno, C., Roux, A., Nelson, M. and Arens, L. (1990) 'Causes of mental handicap in Cape Town', *South African Medical Journal* 77: 98–101

Monaghan, F. (1999) *Defining a Role: the EAL teacher in maths* (Watford: NALDIC)

Office for Standards in Education (Ofsted) (1996) *Exclusions from Secondary Schools 1995–1996* (London: Ofsted)

Office for Standards in Education (Ofsted) (1997) *The Assessment of the Language Development of Bilingual Students* (97/97/NS) (London: Ofsted)

Ofsted and Equal Opportunities Commission (2001) *The Gender Divide*, www.ofsted.gov.uk

Ogbu, J.U. (1978) *Minority Education and Caste* (New York: Academic Press)

Pomplun, M. and Capps, L. (1999) 'Gender differences for constructed response mathematics items', *Educational and Psychological Measurement* 59(4): 597–614

Powers, S. (1996) 'Deaf students' achievements in ordinary schools', *Journal of the British Association of Teachers of the Deaf* 20(4): 111–23

Riddell, S. (1996) 'Gender and special issues in education', in Lloyd, G. (ed) *'Knitting Progress Unsatisfactory': Gender and Special Issues in Education* (Edinburgh: Moray House Publications)

Riddell, S., Brown, S. and Duffield, J. (1994) 'Parental power and special educational needs: the case of specific learning difficulties', *British Educational Research Journal* 20(3): 327–45

Sage, R. (1998) *Evaluation of Dysfluency Courses at the Apple House, Oxford* (Oxford: The Oxford Stammer Trust)

Sage, R. (2000) *The Communication Opportunity Group Scheme* (COGS) (Leicester: The University of Leicester)

Schiff-Myers, N.B. (1992) 'Considering arrested language development and language loss in the assessment of second language learners', *Language, Speech and Hearing Services in Schools* 23: 28–33

Sharma, A. and Love, D. (1991) *A Change in Approach: a report on the experience of deaf people from Black and ethnic minority communities* (London: Royal Association in aid of Deaf People) 1

Shaywitz, S.E., Shaywitz, B.A., Fletcher, J.M. and Escobar, M.D. (1990) 'Prevalence of reading disability in boys and girls: results of the Connecticut Longitudinal Study', *Journal of the American Medical Association* 264: 998–1002

Sheldon, W. H. (1940) *The Varieties of Human Physique* (New York: Harper)

Tanner, J.M. (1970) 'Physical Growth', in Mussen, P.H. (ed) *Carmichaels' Manual of Child Psychology* (Vol. 1) (New York: Wiley)

Tomlinson, S. (1982) *A Sociology of Special Education* (London: Routledge and Kegan Paul) 174

Tomlinson, S. (1984) 'Minority groups in English conurbations', in Williams, P. (ed) *Special Education in Minority Communities* (Milton Keynes: Open University Press)

Tomlinson, S. (1988) 'Why Johnny can't read: critical theory and special education', *European Journal of Special Needs Education* 3(1): 45–58 (a Taylor and Francis Ltd journal – see www.tandf.co.uk/journals/routledge/08856257.html)

Troike, R. (1978) 'Research evidence for the effectiveness of bilingual education', *NABE Journal* 3: 13–24

◆ REFERENCES

Tucker, J.A. (1980) 'Ethnic proportions in classes for the learning disabled: issues in non-biased assessment', *Journal of Special Education* 14: 93–105

Turner, S. (1996) 'Meeting the needs of children under five with sensori-neural hearing loss from ethnic minority families', *Journal of the British Association of Teachers of the Deaf* 20: 91–100

Wadsworth, S.J., De Fries, J.C., Stevenson, J., Gilger, J.W. and Pennington, B.F. (1992) 'Gender ratios among reading-disabled children and their siblings as a function of parental impairment', *Journal of Child Psychology and Psychiatry* 33: 1229–39

Walker, R.N. (1962) 'Body build and behaviour in young children: 1. Body and nursery school teachers' ratings', *Monograph of the Society for Research in Child Development* 27 (Whole No. 84)

Warnock Report (1978) *Special Educational Needs: Report of the Committee of Enquiry into the Education of Handicapped Children and Young People* (London: HMSO)

Willingham, W.W. and Cole, N.S. (1997) *Gender and Fair Assessment* (Mahwah, NJ: Lawrence Erlbaum Associates)

Winter, K. (1999) 'Speech and language therapy provision for bilingual children: aspects of the current service', *International Journal of Language and Communication Disorders* 34(1): 85–98

Wood, R. (1991) *Assessment and Testing: A Survey of Research Commissioned by the University of Cambridge Local Examinations Syndicate* (Cambridge: Cambridge University Press)

Zubrick, A. (1992) 'Child language impairment in Hong Kong', in Fletcher, P. and Hall, D. (eds) *Specific Speech and Language Disorders in Children* (London: Whurr) 135

◆ Chapter Four

Bloom, B.S. (1956) *Taxonomy of Educational Objectives: cognitive domain* (New York: David McKay)

Booth, T. and Ainscow, M. (eds) (1998) *From Them to Us: An international study of inclusion in England* (London: Routledge) 239

Budoff, M. (1987) 'The validity of learning potential assessments', in Lidz, C.S. (ed) *Dynamic Assessment: An interactional approach to evaluating learning potential* (New York: The Guilford Press)

Christenson, S.L. and Ysseldyke J.E. (1989) 'Assessing student performance: an important change is needed', *Journal of School Psychology* 27(4): 409–25

Croll, P. and Moses, D. (1985) *One in Five: The Assessment and Incidence of Special Educational Needs* (London: Routledge and Kegan Paul)

Department for Education and Skills (DfES) (2001) *Special Educational Needs Code of Practice* (London: DfES)

Department of Trade and Industry (DTI) (1995) *Disability Discrimination Act* (London: HMSO)

Elliott, J.G. (2000) 'The psychological assessment of children with learning difficulties', *British Journal of Special Education* 27(2): 59–66

Feuerstein, R. (1979) *The Dynamic Assessment of Retarded Performers: The Learning Potential Assessment Device* (Baltimore, MD: University Park Press)

Frith, U. (1995) 'Dyslexia: can we have a shared theoretical framework?' *Educational and Child Psychology* 12(1): 6–17

Guthke, J., Beckmann, J.F. and Dobat, H. (1997) 'Dynamic testing – problems, uses, trends and evidence of validity', *Educational and Child Psychology* 14(4): 17–32

McKee, W.T. and Witt, J.C. (1990) 'Effective teaching: a review of instructional and environmental variables', in Gutkin, T.B. and Reynolds, C.R. (eds) *The Handbook of School Psychology* (New York: Wiley) 821

Missiuna, C. and Samuels, M. (1988) 'Dynamic assessment: review and critique', *Special Services in the Schools* 5(1,2): 1–22

Qualifications and Curriculum Authority (QCA) (2001) *Curriculum Guidelines for Students with Learning Difficulties* (London: QCA)

Sage, R. (2000a) *The Communication Opportunity Group Scheme* (COGS) (Leicester: The University of Leicester)

Sage, R. (2000b) *Class Talk* (Stafford: Network Educational Press)

Sage, R. (2003) *Assessing and Teaching the Communication Opportunity Group Scheme* (Leicester: University of Leicester)

Sage, R. and Cwenar, S. (2003) *CPD in a School Context: ESCalate Project* (Leicester: The University of Leicester)

Sage, R. and Sommefeldt, D. (2004) *How schools are coping with inclusion* (Leicester: The University of Leicester)

Sternberg, R.J. (1985) *Beyond IQ: A triarchic theory of human intelligence* (Cambridge: Cambridge University Press)

Tomlinson, S. (1988) 'Why Johnny can't read: critical theory and special education', *European Journal of Special Needs Education* 3(1): 10–11 (a Taylor and Francis Ltd journal – see www.tandf.co.uk/journals/routledge/08856257.html)

Vygotsky, L.S. (1978) *Mind and society: The development of higher mental processes* (Cambridge, MA: Harvard University) 85–6

Warnock Report (1978) *Special Educational Needs: Report of the Committee of Enquiry into the Education of Handicapped Children and Young People* (London: HMSO) paragraph 14

Watson, J. (2000) 'Constructive instruction and learning difficulties', *Support for Learning* 15(3): 134–40

Yule, W. (1975) 'Psychological and medical concepts', in Wedell, K. (ed) *Orientation in Special Education* (London: Wiley)

◆ Chapter Five

Ainsworth, M.D.S. (1973) 'The development of infant-mother attachment', in Caldwell, B.M. and Ricciuti, H.N. (eds), *Review of Child Development Research* (Volume 3) (Chicago: University of Chicago Press)

Bandura, A. (1973) *Aggression, A Social Learning Analysis* (Englewood Cliffs, NJ: Prentice Hall)

◆ REFERENCES

Bell, N. (1991) *Visualizing and Verbalizing* (Paso Robles, California: Academy of Reading Publications)

Bell, S.M. (1970) 'The development of the concept of object as related to infant-mother attachment', *Child Development* 41: 291–311

Binet, A. and Simon, T. (1916) *The Development of Intelligence in Children* (Baltimore: Williams and Wilkins)

Borke, H. (1975) 'Piaget's mountains revisited: changes in the egocentric landscape', *Developmental Psychology* 11: 240–3

Bowlby, J. (1969) *Attachment and Loss: Volume 1 Attachment* (New York: Basic Books)

Brazelton, T.B., Robey, J.S. and Collier, G.A. (1969) 'Infant development in the Zinacanteco Indians of southern Mexico', *Pediatrics* 44: 274–93

Bruner, J.S., Olver, R.R. and Greenfield, P.M. (eds) (1966) *Studies in Cognitive Growth* (New York: Wiley)

Chomsky, N. (1965) *Aspects of the Theory of Syntax* (Cambridge, MA: MIT Press)

Cohen, N. (1996) 'Unsuspected language impairments in psychiatrically disturbed children: developmental issues and associated conditions', in Beitchman, J.H., Cohen, N.J., Konstantareas, M.M. and Tannock, R. (eds) *Language, Learning and Behavior Disorders: Developmental, biological and clinical perspectives* (Cambridge: Cambridge University Press)

Cooper, J., Moodley, M. and Reynell, J. (1978) *Helping Language Development* (London: EA Arnold)

Dale, P.S. (1976) *Language Development: Structure and function*, 2nd edn (New York: Holt, Rinehart and Winston)

Diorio, D., Viau,V. and Meaney, M.J. (1993) 'The role of the medial prefrontal cortex in the regulation of hypothalmic-pituitary-adrenal responses to stress', *Journal of Neuroscience* 13.9: 3839–47

Erikson, E.H. (1963) *Childhood and Society* (New York: Norton)

Freire, P. (1972) *Pedagogy of the Oppressed* (London: Penguin)

Freud, S. (1960) *A General Introduction to Psychoanalysis* (New York: Washington Square Press)

Gardner, H. (1993) *Frames of Mind: The theory of multiple intelligences*, 2nd edn (London: Fontana Press)

Gelernter, D. (1994) *The Muse in the Machine, Computerizing the Poetry of Human Thought* (New York: Free Press)

Gesell, A. and Thompson, H. (1929) 'Learning and growth in identical twins: an experimental study by the method of co-twin control', *Genetic Psychology Monographs* 6: 1–123

Gibson, E.J. (1969) *Principles of Perceptual Learning and Development* (New York: Appleton)

Goleman, D. (1996) *Emotional Intelligence* (London: Bloomsbury)

Goodenough, F.L. (1931) *Anger in Young Children* (Minneapolis: University of Minnesota)

Hunter-Carsch, M. (1999) *Report on the Leicester Summer Literacy Scheme* (Leicester: University of Leicester)

Kagan, J. (1965) 'Reflection-impulsivity and reading ability in primary grade children', *Child Development* 609–28

Kagan, J. (1971) *Change and continuity in infancy* (New York: Wiley)

Kohlberg, L. (1966) 'A cognitive-developmental analysis of children's sex-role concepts and attitudes', in Maccoby, E.E. (ed) *The Development of Sex Differences* (Stanford, CA: Stanford University Press)

Levinson, H.N. (1988) 'The cerebellar-vestibular basis of learning disabilities in children, adolescents and adults; hypothesis and study', *Perceptual Motor Skills* 67: 983–1006

Mason, S. (1996) 'Table: 22 Weak Skills in the Workplace', in *Skills and Enterprise Briefing*, 1999 (London: DfEE)

Meadows, S. (1993) *The Child as Thinker: The development and acquisition of cognition in childhood* (London: Routledge)

Merry, R. (1998) *Successful Children, Successful Teaching* (Buckingham: Open University Press)

Merzenich, M. (1995) *Brain Plasticity Origins of Human Abilities and Disabilities*, Sixth Symposium, Decade of the Brain Series, NIMH and the Library of Congress, Washington DC (7 Feb)

Piaget, J. (1964) 'Development and learning', in Ripple, R. and Rockcastle, V. (eds) *Piaget Rediscovered* (Ithaca, NY: Cornell University Press) 7–19

Piaget, J. and Inhelder, B. (1969) *The Psychology of the Child* (New York: Basic Books)

Sage, R. (1990) *A question of language disorder* (unpublished MPhil thesis, The Open University)

Sage, R. (2000a) *The Communication Opportunity Group Scheme* (COGS) (Leicester: The University of Leicester)

Sage, R. (2000b) *Class Talk* (Stafford: Network Educational Press)

Sage, R. (2003) *Lend Us Your Ears* (Stafford: Network Educational Press)

Thomas, A. and Chess, S. (1977) *Temperament and development* (New York: Brunner/Mazel)

Vygotsky, L.S. (1962) *Thought and Language* (New York: Wiley)

Wilde, M. (2004) 'The Communication Opportunity Group Scheme', *Journal of Human Communication International*, 6:1

Williams, J.R. and Scott, R.B. (1953) 'Growth and development of Negro infants: IV. Motor development and its relationships to child rearing practices in two groups of Negro infants', *Child Development*, 24: 103–21

Witkin, H.A., Dyk, R.B., Faterson, H.F., Goodenough, D.R. and Karp, S.A. (1962) *Psychological differentiation* (New York: Wiley)

Wragg, E.C. (1994) *Managing Behaviour* (video and book) (London: BBC Education)

Yarrow, L.J., Rubenstein, J.L., Pedersen, F.A. and Jankowski, J.J. (1972) 'Dimensions of early stimulation and their differential effects on infant development', *Merrill–Palmer Quarterly* 18: 205–18

◆ Chapter Six

Bantock, G.H. (1968) *Culture, Industrialisation and Education* (London: Routledge and Kegan Paul)

Barber, B.R. (1995) *Jihad vs. McWorld* (New York: Times Books)

Boyer, E.L. (1992) *Ready to Learn: A mandate for the nation* (Princeton, NJ: The Carnegie Foundation for the Advancement of Teaching)

Boxall, M. (1996) 'The nurture group in the primary school', in Bennathan, M. and Boxall, M. (eds) *Effective Intervention in Primary Schools: Nurture Groups* (London: David Fulton) 18–38

Brigman, G., Lane, D. and Switzer, D. (1999) 'Teaching children school success skills', *Journal of Educational Research* 92 (6): 323–9

Brown, G., Anderson, A., Shillock, R. and Yule, G. (1984) *Teaching Talk: Strategies for production and assessment* (Cambridge: Cambridge University Press)

Bruner, J. S. (1966) *Toward a Theory of Instruction* (New York: Norton)

Cajkler, W. (1999) 'Misconceptions in the NLS: National Literacy Strategy or No Linguistic Sense?' *Use of English* 50(3): 214–27

Cajkler, W. (2002) 'Literacy Across the Curriculum at KS3: More muddle and confusion', *Use of English* 53(2): 151–64

Cajkler, W. and Hislam, J. (2002) *'The Butler Was Dead' Is Not a Passive Form: How grammar has been misconceived and misapplied in the national curriculum*, Proceedings of the British Educational Research Association, University of Exeter, September: 34

Carr, W. and Hartnett, A. (1996) *Education and the Struggle for Democracy: The politics of educational ideas* (Buckingham: Open University Press)

Cooper, P. (2001) *We Can Work It Out – a review of what works with SEBD* (Barnado's)

Davis, K. and Moore, W.E. (1967) 'Some principles of stratification', in Bendix, R. and Lipset, S.M. (eds) *Class, Status and Power* (London: Kegan Paul)

Dewey, J. (1975) 'The child and the curriculum', in Golby, M., Greenwald, J. and West, R., *Curriculum Design* (London: Croom Helm)

Eco, U. (2001) 'Migration, Tolerance, and the Intolerable', in *Five Moral Questions* (London: Harcourt)

Foucault, M. (1984) *The Foucault Reader* (London: Penguin)

Freire, P. (1972) *Pedagogy of the Oppressed* (London: Penguin

Gardner, H. (1993) *Frames of Mind: The theory of multiple intelligences*, 2nd edn (London: Fontana Press)

Gill, D. and Adams, B. (1989) *ABC of Communication Studies* (London: Macmillan Education)

Handy, C. (1994) *The Empty Raincoat* (London: Arrow Books)

Hillman, J. (1995) *Kinds of Power* (New York: Currency Doubleday)

Illich, I. (1971) *Deschooling Society* (Middlesex: Penguin Education)

Illich, I. (1981) *Shadow Work* (London: Marion Boyars)

Lawton, D. (1999) *Beyond the National Curriculum* (London: Hodder and Stoughton)

Lees, J., Smithies, G. and Chambers, C. (2001) *Let's Talk: a community-based language promotion project for sure start*, in proceedings of the RCSLT National Conference: Sharing Communication, Birmingham, April 2001

Mason, S. (1996) 'Table: 22 Weak Skills in the Workplace', in *Skills and Enterprise Briefing*, 1999 (London: DfEE)

Merry, P. (2000) *Open Source Learning: A key to multiculturalism, citizenship and the knowledge society* (Netherlands: Engage! Interact)

Mobilia, W., Fox, P., Monether, P. and Gordon, R. (2001) *Education by Design: Critical Skills: Level 1 and Level 2* (Stafford: Network Educational Press)

Mosley, J. (1996) *Quality Circle Time* (Wisbech: LDA)

Office for Standards in Education (Ofsted) (2000) *The Annual Report of Her Majesty's Chief Inspector of Schools: Standard and quality in education 1988/99* (London: The Stationery Office) 21

Pate, R.T. and Bremer, N.H. (1967) 'Guiding learning through skilful questioning', *The Elementary School Journal* 67: 417–22

Piaget, P. (1967) *Six Psychological Studies* (London: London University Press)

Robinson, W.P. (1981) 'Language development in young children', in Fontana, D. (ed), *Psychology for Teachers* (London: British Psychological Society and Macmillan)

Sage, R. (2000a) *The Communication Opportunity Group Scheme* (COGS) (Leicester: The University of Leicester)

Sage, R. (2000b) *Class Talk* (Stafford: Network Educational Press)

Sage, R. and Cwenar, S. (2003) *CPD in a School Context: ESCalate Project* (Leicester: University of Leicester)

Sage, R. and Sommefeldt, D. (2004) *How Schools are Coping with Inclusion* (Leicester: The University of Leicester)

Stodolsky, S.S., Ferguson, T.L. And Wimpelberg, K. (1981) 'The recitation persists but what does it look like?', *Journal of Curriculum Studies* 13: 121–30

Teele, S. (2000) *Rainbows of Intelligence: Exploring how children learn* (California: Corwin/Sage) 49

Wilde, M. (2004) 'The Communication Opportunity Group Scheme', *Journal of Human Communication International* 6:1

Wink, W. (1992) *Engaging the Powers – Discernment and resistance in a world of domination* (Minnespolis: Fortress Press)

◆ Appendices

Board of Education (1943) *Norwood Report: Curriculum and examinations in secondary schools* (London: HMSO)

Boxall, M. (1996) 'The nurture group in the primary school', in Bennathan, M. and Boxall, M. (eds) *Effective Intervention in Primary Schools: Nurture groups* (London: David Fulton) 18–38

Dearing, R. (chair)(1994) *The Final Report: The National Curriculum and its assessment* (London: SCAA)

Department for Education and Employment (DfEE) (1997) Green Paper: *Excellence for All Children* (London: DfEE)

Department for Education and Science (DES) (1989) *The Task Group on Assessment and Testing: A report* (London: HMSO)

Gipps, C. and Stobart, G. (1993) *Assessment* (London: Hodder and Stoughton)

Mann, J.F. (1979) *Education* (London: Pitman)

Mobilia, W., Fox, P., Monether, P. and Gordon, R. (2001) *Education by Design: Critical Skills: Level 1 and Level 2* (Stafford: Network Educational Press) (see also www.criticalskills.co.uk)

Mosley, J. (1996) *Quality Circle Time* (Wisbech: LDA)

Nelson, D. and Burchell, K. (1998) *Evaluation of the Communication Opportunity Group Scheme* (Warwick: South Warwickshire Combined Care NHS Trust, Dept of Speech and language Therapy)

Sage, R. (2000) *The Communication Opportunity Group Scheme* (COGS) (Leicester: The University of Leicester)

Sage, R. (2003) *Lend Us Your Ears* (Stafford: Network Educational Press)

Sage, R. and Sommefeldt, D. (2004) *An Evaluation of Inclusion in Leicester Schools* (Leicester: The University of Leicester)

Trew, M. (1999) 'A report on the use of Jenny Mosley's whole-school Quality Circle Time model in primary schools in the UK' (published by the author)

Weatherley, C. (2000) *Leading the Learning School* (Stafford: Network Educational Press)

Weatherley, C., Bonney, B., Kerr, J. and Morrison, J. (2002) *Transforming Teaching and Learning* (Stafford: Network Educational Press)

Westby, C. (1984) 'Development of narrative language abilities', in Wallach, G.P. and Butler, K.G. (eds) *Language Learning Disabilities in School-age Children* (Baltimore, MD: Williams and Wilkins) 103–27

Young, M.F.D. (1998) *The Curriculum of the Future: From the new sociology of education to a critical theory of learning* (London: Falmer Press)

◆ Index